The Kids' OUTDOOR ADVENTURE Book
448 Great Things to Do in Nature Before You Grow Up

Stacy Tornio and Ken Keffer

Illustrations by Rachel Riordan

FALCONGUIDES

GUILFORD, CONNECTICUT
HELENA, MONTANA
AN IMPRINT OF GLOBE PEQUOT PRESS

FALCONGUIDES®

Copyright © 2013 by Stacy Tornio and Ken Keffer

FalconGuides® is an imprint of Globe Pequot Press.

Falcon, FalconGuides, and Outfit Your Mind are registered trademarks of Morris Book Publishing, LLC.

Illustrations by Rachel Riordan © 2013 by Morris Book Publishing, LLC
Text Design: Sheryl P. Kober
Project Editor: Tracee Williams
Layout: Maggie Peterson

Library of Congress Cataloging-in-Publication Data

Tornio, Stacy.
 The kids' outdoor adventure book : 448 great things to do in nature before you grow up / Stacy Tornio and Ken Keffer ; illustrations by Rachel Riordan.
     p. cm.
 Includes index.
 ISBN 978-0-7627-8352-6
 1. Outdoor recreation—Juvenile literature. 2. Nature—Juvenile literature. I. Keffer, Ken. II. Riordan, Rachel, ill. III. Title.
 GV191.62.T67 2013
 796.5—dc23

                                                        2012037202

Printed in the United States of America

10 9 8 7 6 5 4

To Jack and Annabelle, for encouraging me not to be a wuss. —ST

To my parents. Ma, thanks for teaching me how to fish,
and Pa, thanks for teaching me how to hunt. —KCK

Contents

Acknowledgments

Thank you Ian for giving us inspiration.

Thanks to our wonderful agent Uwe Stender of TriadaUS for believing in this book from the very beginning. And thanks to our editor Katie Benoit Cardoso for instantly seeing our vision to get more kids outside. You've been a dream to work with, and this book is better thanks to you and the entire FalconGuides team at Globe Pequot Press.

Thanks to Steve Tornio for always listening to our ideas. Though we didn't take all of your advice (like calling the book *Nature's Death Match*), you've been an incredible resource throughout it all.

Thanks to Rachel Riordan. We can't imagine *The Kids' Outdoor Adventure Book* without your festive, whimsical illustrations.

Finally, this book wouldn't even exist without some pretty amazing nature people influencing our own lives when we were growing up. They helped us appreciate the great outdoors, and they showed us how to pass it on to others. So thank you Roland and Linda Lancaster, Grandpa and Grandma Bingham, Grandpa and Grandma Ritchie, Grandpa and Grandma Keffer, Steve and Montana Lancaster, Preston Keffer, Uncle Larry and Aunt Kathy, Mark-o and Gwyn-o, and Scott Schaefer.

Foreword

If you picked up this book to share with your kids, you likely grew up in the 1970s or '80s like me. We were part of the first generation of kids that had home video games, first Atari, then Sega and Nintendo. We were the first kids to have both hundreds of cable television channels and home computers as entertainment options in our homes. When our generation went to high school and then college in the 1990s, we were the first to have personal laptops and cell phones, and the first to have limitless information and distraction at our fingertips via the Internet.

And yet, we still played outside as kids. I built forts, caught frogs in the creek in the woods behind my house, and climbed trees, and my friends and I invented outdoor games using nothing more than our own creativity. I played outside until it got dark (sometimes even after that) or until my mom called me to come inside. Even in high school in the 1990s, I'd hang out at the park or the beach with my friends, and in college we'd go camping or hiking for fun.

Our generation might be the last to have outdoor time as a daily part of our lives. When we were kids, despite the exciting new technologies, electronic games and media hadn't yet dominated our time or become the artificial babysitters they are today. Parents didn't feel the need to schedule every waking moment of our time, and didn't think twice about sending us outside to play. In high school and college we didn't have blogs to read or Facebook updates to obsessively post.

The nature of childhood has changed, and the sad reality is that there's not much nature left in it.

Today in America, the average school-aged kid spends almost eight hours a day indoors in front of electronic media, sedentary. By the time a child goes to kindergarten, he or she has already watched five thousand hours of television. At the same time, childhood obesity rates have skyrocketed, childhood diabetes is on the rise, and most kids can now name more corporate logos than they can tree or bird species that live in their own neighborhoods. If this doesn't frighten you, it should.

Technology isn't inherently bad, but most would agree that its dominance in the lives of today's children—at the expense of outdoor time—is way out of a healthy balance. Similarly, modern parents' obsession with scheduling every second of their kids' time in structured activities has resulted in burned out kids who never get to just run around and be kids.

That's the bad news.

The good news is that we can do something about it. We can reverse the unhealthy trend of overscheduled "indoor kids."

There are a growing number of studies that all conclude the same thing: Kids who regularly spend time outside, particularly those who get unstructured outdoor play time, are healthier. "Outdoor kids" are less likely to be obese or to have diabetes. Kids who go outside are less likely to be near-sighted or deficient in vitamin D. They're less likely to suffer from allergies. Outdoor time has been shown to have positive effects on kids struggling with attention deficit issues. Spending time outside can even help kids' classroom performance; in a survey of more than two thousand educators conducted by my colleagues here at the National Wildlife Federation, the majority of teachers reported that outdoor time led to better focus in the classroom, increased learning, and even better test scores. Kids who engage in outdoor play and exploration exercise not only their bodies, but also their creativity and their decision and leadership skills.

As parents, how our kids spend their time is up to us. Sometimes it's as simple as making outdoor time a priority in our busy schedules. Sometimes it means limiting the time our kids spend online, watching television, or playing video games, even if that means we must use the dreaded "no." Sometimes it means leaving work on time, or turning our own electronics off on the weekend so we can make sure our kids get to play outside and be kids. We have the power to reverse the indoor kid trend and all of its negative consequences.

You hold in your hands a wonderful resource in accomplishing just that. *The Kids' Outdoor Adventure Book* makes it easy to give your kids that critical outdoor time. Stacy Tornio and Ken Keffer have done a phenomenal job of collecting fun outdoor activities that kids of all ages can enjoy.

The Kids' Outdoor Adventure Book is organized by season and is filled with checklists, games, challenges, and projects. You don't have to read this book cover-to-cover to be able to use it; simply open a page and go with it. The activities are written with simple, easy-to-understand instructions, keeping the busy schedules of adults in mind. You don't have to be a naturalist to create great outdoor experiences for your kids. Stacy and Ken have done all the hard work for you!

And here at the National Wildlife Federation, we know the old saying "you only protect what you love, and you only love what you know" is true. The thought of the next generation—our kids—growing up into adults who don't care about protecting wilderness areas, about keeping our air and water clean, or about saving wildlife because they had no opportunity as a child to experience the natural world around them is a scary prospect.

This book is a key to ensuring that doesn't happen.

David Mizejewski
Naturalist and Media Personality
National Wildlife Federation

Introduction

It all started on a boat with Stacy and her nephew Ian.

"Before I grow up, I want to jump off this boat into the middle of the lake," Ian said. "It's on my list."

He was nine at the time.

We were fascinated with Ian's notion of having a list of things he wanted to accomplish before he reached adulthood. Better yet, it had to do with nature. It wasn't a list about which video game he wanted to conquer or what TV show he wanted to watch—it was a checklist for nature.

Inspired by Ian and just for fun, we started making our own list. We wrote down all the fun things in nature that kids should try—we drew from personal experience, chatted with friends, and talked to kids. The ideas were endless.

Learn how to skip rocks.
Milk a cow.
Try fly fishing.
Grow your own veggies.
Paddle a canoe.
Catch a frog.
Find a bird's nest.

We knew we were onto something and eventually came up with 448 ideas total. After all, organizations like the National Wildlife Federation and the Earth Day Network have been encouraging parents to "get kids outside" for years. But in a world of electronics and busy family schedules, the outdoors often drops a few notches on the priority list.

Richard Louv brought this message back into the forefront with his book, *Last Child in the Woods,* in 2005. Louv's hope and vision is that no child gets left inside. It's a worthy goal. Recent studies show that kids who play outside are healthier, happier, and more well rounded as a whole. The potential rewards just for getting kids outside seem endless. From reducing childhood obesity to preserving our natural resources, it opens up dozens of possibilities to create powerful chain reactions.

But take a step back for a moment. This is all well and good, but it's pretty overwhelming for today's modern family, moving ninety miles an hour just trying to stay afloat among all the requirements of life.

This is where we are making it simple.

This book isn't about why it's important to get kids outside. Nor is it filled with reasons you should. After all, we know being outside and in nature is a good thing. You know it's a good thing, too, or you wouldn't be reading this right now. In addition, this book isn't trying to compete with electronics, video games, and technology. We don't believe it's an either/or situation. We live in a world filled with technology, yet we're surrounded by nature. We believe the two can coexist. The two must coexist.

So what is this book about? In its simplest form, it's about celebrating the great outdoors and all it has to offer. It's about remembering what it's like when someone tells you to "go outside and play" and you create your own fun. It's about discovering the awe of something in nature for the first time, the second time, or even the 102nd time. And it's about connecting with Mother Nature as a family.

Nature is a destination, but you don't have to travel anywhere to find it. Just open the door and step outside. The tiniest of porches can house a flower container. A backyard can provide a lifetime of natural experiences. Nature is everywhere. From sea to sea. From backyard to mountaintop.

The Kids' Outdoor Adventure Book can be read page by page as a family, checking off list items as you accomplish them and making a list of things you want to try. Or maybe you use the book to inspire—when you're looking for something to do. Open it up to a random page and take your pick. With 448 items and an adventure scale listed for all the checklist items, there are activities for both new and experienced nature lovers.

We've organized *The Kids' Outdoor Adventure Book* to be as easy and friendly as possible and perfect for kids thirteen and under to do with their family. We even have an adventure scale, so there really is something for everyone. The book is divided by season, with fifty checklist items (and a challenge for each item) anchoring each section. Then throughout each season, you'll find expanded ideas for getting involved in nature with featured projects, destinations, and foods from the garden (with recipes to try). Finally, we have plenty of fascinating facts, useful tips, game ideas, and more. You're guaranteed to learn a thing or two about nature along the way!

We hope *The Kids' Outdoor Adventure Book* helps you discover places, hobbies, and things in the great outdoors that you've never experienced before. And we hope it inspires you to create your own list, just like Ian did, for the things you want to accomplish outside.

By the way, Ian did end up taking a leap off the boat that day, and in his own words, "It was awesome!"

So go ahead and jump into the season you're in right now to get started. It's time to get outside.

Psst Kids!

These couple of pages are basically telling your parents this—nature is awesome. But you already know nature is awesome, don't you? So go outside! Please get your parents outside as much as possible. They might need it more than you!

How to Use This Book

The Kids' Outdoor Adventure Book is easy to use. You don't have to start at the beginning of the book. What season are you in right now? Flip to any page in that season and you'll find something fun to do today. You can go page by page or pick out your favorites to try.

The Kids' Outdoor Adventure Book includes 448 things to do in nature for kids of all ages. That is more than one activity for every single day of the year. The book is broken down by season. Each season features fifty checklist items, fifty challenge items, three projects, three destinations, three garden recipes, and three outdoor games. Throughout the book, you'll also find fascinating facts, useful tips and tricks, and plenty of additional resources to turn to.

200 Checklist Items

What are your favorite things to do outside? Our favorites are highlighted here. Each item has an adventure rating from 1 being the easiest to 5 being the hardest.

200 Checklist Challenges

Challenges go beyond the basic checklist item to help you dig a little deeper into nature.

12 Projects

Featured projects focus on natural or recycled materials. Estimated times are given for each project as well as suggested ages.

12 Destinations

While nature is everywhere, you can't experience all nature has to offer in your own backyard. You won't have to travel too far though for these destinations.

12 Featured Foods

Beyond simple recipes, *The Kids' Outdoor Adventure Book* introduces you to techniques to make the most of your backyard harvest and beyond.

12 Outdoor Games

Go outside and play. It is as simple as that. Classic childhood games are highlighted. Grab some friends and let the games begin.

SPRING

 Spring is definitely the best season. Think about it—it's the ultimate season for new life. And it's the perfect time to go out and experience it firsthand. The days are getting longer, and there is always fun to be had. It's time to shed the winter coat and throw on a light spring jacket instead.

Everything seems a bit brighter in spring as winter fades away. Lingering traces of cold are replaced with warmer weather. Spring rain showers come and go, helping to turn the landscape green. Nothing is finer than the aftermath of a spring rain—the smells, chirping birds, droplets of water lingering on tulips. Pretty soon, the tree leaves will quickly fill in the canopies. As the ground thaws, gardeners start digging in the dirt again, hopeful their efforts will pay off in gorgeous blooms. Veggie gardens are planted with the promise of bountiful produce in summer while early garden harvests like asparagus and strawberries liven up the dinner table.

Frogs and toads belt out the season with boisterous calls. Hibernating animals emerge, ready for a snack after a long winter. Birds return on migration journeys from across the globe, each day bringing new arrivals. Some species just stop to rest and refuel, while others stick around, building nests and raising families. Meanwhile family farms become nurseries in the spring with baby calves, lambs, foals, and piglets taking their first steps on wobbly legs.

Spring is the season to dust off your bicycle and unpack much of your outdoor gear. Getting reacquainted with spring is like seeing a friend you haven't seen in a long time. You are so excited to catch up, and it instantly feels like you were never apart.

Spring adventure awaits. Just open the door, step outside, and let the fun begin.

Spring's Checklist

1: Watch the Clouds Float By
ADVENTURE SCALE: 1

The basics: This is a great activity to do at the end of a busy day. Just lie back, relax, and watch the clouds roll on by. Clouds are one of those little things in nature that you don't notice every day, but if you sit back and look, you'll realize how beautiful they really are.

Challenge: Find animal shapes in those clouds. Maybe one looks like a bird or perhaps a butterfly in the sky—let your imagination be your guide. And if you're with a friend, play I Spy in the clouds.

Did you know: Clouds are made up of teeny tiny droplets of water and ice. When these tiny droplets become too heavy, it rains. So even though these clouds might look like you could sit on them, you'd fall right through.

2: Watch the Tide Come In
ADVENTURE SCALE: 2

The basics: Go to the beach in the evening, and just wait for the tide to come in. It's impressive to see the water splash up higher and higher on the beach, and it's fun to run through the edge of the waves too.

Challenge: Watch the tide go out in the morning, and find a tide pool to explore. Tide pools are where pockets of water gather and sea creatures like to live. Horseshoe crabs are one thing you might spot. Go see what else you can find.

Did you know: The tide comes in twice a day: morning and evening. Why? It's because of the gravitational pull of the earth. And since the earth rotates, you get it twice. Try timing the tide coming in to see how long it takes. It happens a lot faster than most people think.

3: Catch a Frog or Toad
ADVENTURE SCALE: 3

The basics: Most frogs and toads like to be near water, so that's a good place to start looking if you're trying to catch one. When you find a frog or a toad, be gentle with it and then let it go.

Challenge: Build a toad abode for your little friend. Make one using an old terra-cotta pot or container. Make sure to leave an opening so the toad can come and go as he pleases. You can even decorate the outside area with rocks and such to make it more like a natural setting.

Did you know: Frogs and toads are not the same thing at all—they even come from different scientific families. Frogs have bulging eyes and webbed feet. (These are just a couple of differences. Look up more online or in a book.) Toads have stubby legs, short hind feet, and often have dry, warty skin. But don't worry—you're not going to get warts from them. This is a myth!

4: Run Barefoot on the Beach
ADVENTURE SCALE: 1

The basics: It's pretty simple—find an open stretch of beach and just take off running. You'll love the feel of the sand between your toes. Don't worry if you quickly have to stop after you start. It's hard work running in the sand. For easier running, get closer to the water where the sand is more firm.

Challenge: Have a crab race with your friends. You know how to walk like a crab? Get down on all fours with your belly facing the sky. Ready, set, go!

Discover more: Even if you don't live somewhere that borders an ocean, there are still beaches around. Go to your regional or state travel website and do a search for "beach." Even small, man-made lakes have great beaches. They even bring nice sand in to get a real beach feel.

PUBLIC BEACHES

Ah, the beach. It's one of the most sought-after destinations in the world. Nothing seems to make people happier than sitting with their toes in the sand, staring out at blue-green water. So what are you waiting for? Get out there and hit the beach this season!

WHO? You can be any age to enjoy the beach because you can pretty much do anything while you're there. Young kids will just like sitting in the sand with a shovel and some toys while older kids will definitely want to hit the water. Best of all, you can set up your chairs or umbrella anywhere and be close to all the action.

WHAT? Don't think the beach is just about sitting around. There are lots of activities to do—from swimming and building sandcastles to playing volleyball and Frisbee. You can also bring a picnic lunch, rent equipment from area vendors, or take your bike or in-line skates for a beachfront ride. This doesn't even include some of the classic beach to-dos, like waiting for the tide to come in, burying your feet in the sand, or looking for seashells.

WHEN? Many people think of the beach as a summertime activity, but spring is actually ideal in a lot of locations. If you're in the South, a beach trip can be the perfect weekend springtime getaway before it gets too hot and crowded. Be sure to check out the beach in all seasons too. People often overlook beaches when it's not warm and sunny out, but these are ideal days to go. It's less crowded overall, and you can appreciate the natural, simple beauty of the area instead.

WHERE? You can find great beaches all over the country. While the East, West, and Gulf Coasts are great places to start, don't be limited by those alone. You can also find great beaches along the shores of the Great Lakes—

or any lakes for that matter. Scope out some beaches near you—and pay them a visit this spring. Even if they're not in full swing until summer, it's a great time to become familiar with them and check out the wildlife nearby.

WHY? The beach is filled with sea and water life that you might not otherwise come into contact with. Don't forget about this precious resource, and share it with a friend. You're bound to discover something new with each and every visit.

Tips and Tricks

While it's great to go to the beach on a hot, busy day, it's even better to go when there aren't a lot of people around. If this means checking it out on a cloudy day or early in the morning, go for it. During these times, you'll gain a better understanding and appreciation for the nature life in that area.

5: Make Leaf Prints

ADVENTURE SCALE: 3

The basics: First things first—go out and collect a few leaves from trees and shrubs. These new spring leaves will be sturdy and perfect for making prints. Next, pour your favorite paint on a plate and gently dip the leaves into the paint. Press the dipped leaf firmly on a blank piece of paper to make your print. Repeat with as many leaves and paint colors as you want.

Challenge: Create a leaf-print container using a terra cotta pot and a paint that's made to go outside (the Patio Paint brand works well, and you can buy it at local craft stores). Press the leaves covered with paint firmly on the outside of the terra cotta pot. Let dry and then add plants.

Did you know: Here's another way to make a leaf print: Place a piece of paper over a leaf. Then unwrap your favorite crayon and turn it on its side. Gently roll with it back and forth until you see the shape coming through.

6: Pick Your Own Bouquet

ADVENTURE SCALE: 2

The basics: Look to your own backyard for inspiration on picking your own bouquet. Try coneflowers, daisies, and black-eyed susans. After you've picked the flowers, be creative with filler plants. Evergreens and ornamental grasses are both great accent pieces. Remember that most wildflowers you see around are protected, and you're not supposed to pick them. So ask first before picking if it's not in your own backyard.

Challenge: Find a nearby "pick-your-own" place to visit. Yes, there are pick-your-own flower places all over the country. Even if it's a little ways out, it'll still be worth the drive. And these bouquets make for great gifts.

Did you know: Want to make your cut flowers last longer? After a couple of days, trim the ends of the stems again and add fresh water. This will help keep them going even longer.

7: Keep a Journal of "Firsts"

ADVENTURE SCALE: 4

The basics: This one sounds like it might be easy, but it can actually take a bit of work. It has a cool payoff if you keep after it, though. Make a list of nature "firsts" like first robin to show up in the backyard, first grasshopper you see, first tulip to bloom, first day to ride your bike outside in spring, etc. Write down the date and any other details that are important. Then in a year, you can read back in your journal and compare dates from one year to the next. It's a bit of a science experiment and journal all rolled into one.

Challenge: Take pictures of as many "firsts" as you can and add them to your journal. Then you can see how one year differs from the next. Be sure to take pictures of yourself as well, so you can see how you change from one year to the next too.

Discover more: Instead of writing a traditional journal, try taking it online. Blogger.com and wordpress.com are both good blogging tools, and you can set them to be public or private.

8: Go to a Hot Air Balloon Festival

ADVENTURE SCALE: 2

The basics: Spring is a popular time for hot air balloon festivals. These festivals have been around for decades, and the balloons are just as impressive today as they ever were. It's amazing to see a hot air balloon up close, and watch it floating through the sky on a sunny day.

Challenge: Ride in a hot air balloon. If you're the adventurous type and you're not scared of heights, this is perfect for you. This can be expensive, but if it's a dream, save up your money and do it.

Did you know: Hot air balloons work because warm air rises in cooler air. So there's a gas burner on each balloon (similar to the gas burner that powers an outdoor grill) to make it work. While you're at a festival, see if they'll show you how it works. It's pretty cool!

NATURE SCRAPBOOK

From the first sunny day of spring to the last big flakes of snow falling in winter—sometimes nature is so impressive that you just want to capture it. With a scrapbook, you can! Gather up some of your favorite photos from outside or use it as an excuse to go out and take some new ones.

Supplies: Scrapbook, camera, glue, markers
Ages: Any age
Time: 30 minutes

How-To:

1. If you already have some photos that you took, gather them up and decide how you want to group them together. Do you have flower photos that you want on the first few pages? Do you want to organize it by season? Don't worry if you don't have everything figured out right away—you can always change or add on later.
2. Find a scrapbook at a local craft store that's a good fit for how many pages you want to have. You can also make your own scrapbook by putting colored pages together or taking a plain blank-paged journal and covering it with a fun design.
3. Don't spend a lot of extra money on cute stickers and designed cutouts. Make your own instead! Also look at old calendars, magazines, and even books you can pick up at rummage sales and thrift stores for inspiration.
4. Add a border to your pictures if you'd like, and then glue your pictures on to the new pages.
5. Don't forget to write a little note or journal entry for the picture, especially if you took it in or around your backyard. You might think you'll remember the picture now, but you might not. So take a little extra time to write about it now, and even add a date. Next year at this time when you're looking at it, it'll be nice to have.

6. Add to the scrapbook as you see fit, and use it as inspiration to go outside and explore more.

Tips and Tricks

If you're keeping a scrapbook or journal, consider adding an entry each week for an entire year, starting with the first day of spring. It's a good way to see what's happening in your own backyard year-round. Also, give it a theme. Maybe instead of one huge scrapbook, you'd like to keep separate ones for the flowers you see, the bugs, wildlife, etc.

pansies from my garden

9: Listen to the Night Sounds

ADVENTURE SCALE: 2

The basics: This is the perfect excuse to stay up late. Wait until it's completely dark out, and then go outside and just listen to the sounds of the night. What will you hear—an owl, crickets, toads, wolves? See if you can pick out the different sounds and figure out what they are.

Challenge: You can hear them, but can you see them? Try to spot one of these critters making the sounds as well. They often get quiet when you shine a light, so you might have to be a little sneaky. Practice seeing things in the dark. Once your eyes adjust, it's pretty easy.

Did you know: Toads don't just croak. They also squeak. If you catch a toad, hold it up and listen closely to see if you hear it squeak as well.

10: Find a Four-Leaf Clover

ADVENTURE SCALE: 4

The basics: To find a patch of clover, lie down in the grass and get really comfortable. Ready? Let the searching begin. Four-leaf clovers are rare to find, so don't expect to uncover one right away. But if you pay close attention, your efforts could pay off and you might have a little luck coming your way!

Challenge: Why stop at just one? You don't want your luck to run out. See if you can find two four-leaf clovers. You could even give one to a friend to bring a little luck her way. What a great gift!

Did you know: Traditionally, four-leaf clovers are pretty rare—only one in about ten thousand plants will have one. However, some growers are developing plants that will produce even more four-leaf clovers. Ask around at your local garden center if you want to plant some. Either way, though, it's still a lucky find. So keep on searching.

OUTDOOR SCAVENGER HUNT

Ages: 5 and up
Materials: Paper, pen, prize
Length: 15 minutes
Number of players: 2 or more

It's a blast to create your own scavenger hunt. Whether you're creating the clues for someone else or are going on the hunt yourself, it's a fun way to get outside. Be sure to mix the clues up, and don't make them too easy. Remember, make 'em work for it.

1. Create your own fun by putting together an outdoor scavenger hunt for your brother, sister, friends, or even parents. First, every good scavenger hunt needs a good prize to find at the end. It doesn't have to cost a lot of money. It can be something small like a drawing, a poem, or even a little piece of candy. But it's definitely more fun to have something at the end to reward you.
2. To get ready for the hunt, you need to write good clues. Make sure every clue points players to something specific outside. For example, a clue like "look under a tree" isn't as effective as "look under this tree where the red birdhouse hangs." Place the next clue under this tree, and so on and so forth.
3. Create at least 10 to 20 clues total. The hunt part will go fast, so even if it feels like you have a lot done, do a few more.
4. Number them as you go so when you're setting out the clues, you won't get mixed up from one to the next (make sure no one is looking). Don't forget to set aside the first clue for the players. They need something to get started.
5. Place your prize at the end, after the very last clue. You can put something on the last clue pointing the players to the treasure.
6. Once all your clues are in place, you're all ready. Give your players the first clue, and then let them be off.

Tip
Adjust your clues to your audience. If you have younger kids doing the hunt, you'll want to make them easier. If you have older kids, make it harder. If you really want a challenge, try to write your clues so they all rhyme.

11: Wake Up before the Birds

ADVENTURE SCALE: 2

The basics: You've heard the phrase the early bird catches the worm, right? Well, the early birder hears the birds. The dawn chorus of bird songs is an experience anyone can appreciate. While it's mostly males singing during this time to proclaim a territory or attract a mate, females of certain species (like vireos or cardinals) will also add to the chorus line.

Challenge: Bird songs can be fun to learn, but don't get overwhelmed. Set a goal to learn songs from ten to twenty species of common birds in your area. It will add fun to your day, and spring is the perfect time to learn them.

Discover more: Cornell Lab of Ornithology has some of the best bird songs around. Go on their website, allaboutbirds.org, where you can find bird profiles and listen to their songs. The songs and calls on here are real recordings from nature.

12: Celebrate Earth Day

ADVENTURE SCALE: 2

The basics: Earth Day, April 22, is one of the most celebrated nature days all year. You're bound to find places in your area celebrating this iconic day. Go to a pre-planned celebration, or create your own by exploring your own backyard and neighborhood. The bottom line is—get outside!

Challenge: Another iconic nature celebration is Arbor Day, held the last Friday in April. Plant a tree on Arbor Day and watch it grow year after year. If you don't have room to plant a tree yourself, see if you can plant one in a local park or somewhere else to support your local community.

Discover more: Earth Day gets bigger and better every single year. See how you can be involved on a local level by going to earthday.org. If there's nothing scheduled, see if you can put something together at your school or library. They'd probably love to have someone get something going.

13: Raft down a River

ADVENTURE SCALE: 4

The basics: A leisurely rafting trip is a lot of fun, and you can even fit the whole family in the same boat or raft if you plan it right. Either enjoy the river ride as a passenger or grab a paddle and help navigate the water. But make sure to take a minute to check out your surroundings. Floating down a river gives you a new perspective on nature and wildlife.

Challenge: Hold on tight and raft through some whitewater rapids (with the proper safety gear on, of course). You might want to check on the river's level of difficulty before you commit, but there are hundreds of options all across the country.

Did you know: Whitewater rafting is actually considered a competitive sport. So if you really love it, keep practicing. You could be on the national team.

SMOOTHIES

Nothing says warmer days are ahead than a fresh smoothie. Make your own using just a few ingredients. They're naturally healthy and delicious, and it's a great way to use up those extra berries you've picked from the garden or have from the farmers' market.

Strawberry Banana Smoothie Serving size: 2–3
2 cups frozen yogurt (strawberry or vanilla)
1 cup fresh strawberries
1 banana
1/2 cup ice

Mix all ingredients in a blender. If too runny, add a few more strawberries. Serve immediately. You can also add in blueberries and/or pineapple if you'd like, but this is a good base.

Tropical Smoothie Serving size: 2–3
1 cup frozen yogurt
1 1/2 cups mango
1/2 cup fresh or frozen peaches
1/2 cup pineapple juice
1/2 cup ice

Mix all ingredients in blender. If you want your smoothie to be thicker, add some ice. Serve immediately.

Mixed Berry Smoothie Serving size: 2-3

1 cup frozen yogurt
1/2 cup blueberries
1/2 cup strawberries
1/4 cup blackberries
1/4 cup raspberries
1/2 cup cherry juice
1/2 cup ice

Mix all ingredients in blender. Mix and match the berries as much as you want. If you like a lot of blackberries but don't like blueberries, change it out. The same goes for the juice—you can try apple or cranberry juice instead. Add ice to thicken the consistency, and serve immediately.

Tips and Tricks

If you go to pick berries this spring at any of the pick-your-own farms, be sure to pick some extras to freeze. They are easy to store, and they are great for using in smoothies. Also, mix and match as much as you want. Don't have frozen yogurt? Try any flavor of regular yogurt instead. Don't have the exact fruit or juice listed? Try something else. You might find you come up with a brand new recipe.

14: Find at Least Five New Animals in the Wild

ADVENTURE SCALE: 5

The basics: There are all kinds of animals out there, and most of the time, you just need to look. Do a little research and make a list of animals that are in your area. Then set a goal to find at least five new ones this spring. Animals that might be on your list could include opossum, raccoon, beaver, porcupine, bear, deer, and more. Remember to keep your distance, and respect the animal's habitat.

Challenge: Don't stop at just five. Challenge yourself to see at least twenty new animals this spring. This will really make you get outside and explore beyond your own backyard. Keep a journal to keep track of your sightings.

Discover more: The Kaufman Field Guide series is one of the best around. Look for the *Field Guide to Mammals of North America* and *Field Guide to Birds of North America*. The books are friendly, compact, and useful. Learn more at kaufmanfieldguides.com or Falcon.com

15: Collect Seashells

ADVENTURE SCALE: 2

The basics: Searching for seashells is probably one of the most popular beach activities of all time. The best thing about it is that you never know what will turn up, because the tide uncovers or washes up new treasures every day. Go out early in the morning before the beaches have been picked over for the best results.

Challenge: Learn how to identify at least five different seashells. Look online for a good resource on shell identification or pick up a book at your local library. It's fun to know what you're looking for.

Did you know: Most seashells you find on the beach were living creatures at some point. The next time you're at an aquarium, see if you can spot a starfish. Sea creatures are often softer than you'd imagine, as is the case with the starfish. Then when it dies, it dries out on the beach and gets hard.

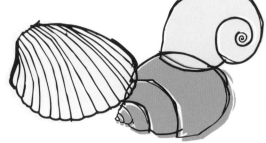

16: Find a Bird's Nest

ADVENTURE SCALE: 3

The basics: As the days get longer, migratory birds return north for the breeding season. If you pay attention, there's a good chance you'll spot birds building a nest out of sticks, grass, hair, or even spider webs. A handful of backyard birds will use birdhouses while others build their nests anywhere they can, including trees, hanging baskets, and even the tops of lampposts.

Challenge: Put up a birdhouse this year and see what you attract (try our vintage bird-house project on page 38). And if you want to take it one step further, monitor the nests by keeping a journal and making notes of how the fledglings grow.

Bonus video: Some birds nest high while others nest low. Others even nest in silly places like lampposts. Get tips on how to find a bird's nest at destinationnature.net.

FOUR-SEASON GARDEN

Plant a garden in spring that will still look good in winter. Yes, it really is possible. It just takes a little research and planning. Here's how to get a garden that you can enjoy in all four seasons.

Supplies: Seeds, plants, soil (if needed)
Ages: Any age
Time: 1 hour

How-To:

1. To kick things off, you need a spot for your garden. If you don't already have a space cleared and ready for planting, get to work. You can till up a fresh area, put in a raised bed, or even create an area with several containers. You don't need a huge space—it can be as big or small as you want.
2. If needed, fill your new planting area with soil. Try mixing in a little organic matter on top to get your garden started off on the right foot.
3. Now for the planning—it's best to create a plan now for the whole season so you can be sure to have something blooming (or to eat) at all times. You can also make a calendar. Then you'll know exactly when to plant your next round.
4. Once you know which plants you're going to plant, dig in as early as possible in spring. While you're planting, keep in mind that you'll be adding along the way. You might even want to make a little diagram so you'll know what should go where.
5. Take good care of your plants. Keep them watered, and make sure the weeds stay out. This will help ensure they live a long life.
6. Keep an eye on your calendar, and when it's time to plant new seeds or add a new season of plants, get them in the ground as soon as you can.

Here's a Good Planting Plan to Get You a Four-Season Garden:

Spring: Plant pansies along the front edge, ornamental grasses in the back, and carrots in the middle. You'll enjoy the pretty colors all spring. Then in early summer, you'll start to get carrots.

Summer: In early summer, add in some native perennials like coneflowers or blanket flower just in front of the grasses. After you've pulled up all your carrots, replace the space with a couple of pumpkin seeds. Remember pumpkins are vines and need room to grow, but if you get these in by mid-summer, you'll have your own jack-o-lantern in October.

Fall: The perennials might not have flowers their first year, but now they're good and established for next year. After you pick your pumpkins, it's time to plant your garlic. It will stay in the garden over winter and come up in spring. If you don't want to plant garlic, plant tulip bulbs instead.

Winter: Now is the time to admire the beauty of your frozen garden. The ornamental grasses and perennials look great in the garden, and they can still be a food source for birds. Even though it's cold out, your garden can still look great.

Tips and Tricks
When planning your garden, ask yourself certain questions. Do you want to have things you can eat? Do you mostly like flowers? How big of a space do the plants require? When do these plants bloom? Do they need sun or shade? These are all factors you should consider.

17: Start Your Own Plants from Seeds

ADVENTURE SCALE: 3

The basics: As winter shifts to spring, it's time to start your new garden for the season. Get going weeks earlier (instead of waiting for the chance of frost to pass) by starting your own seeds inside. For optimal success, be sure to follow the instructions on the back of the seed packet, and make sure your plants get enough sunlight. (See our helpful tips from our four-season garden project on page 18.)

Challenge: Instead of buying a seedlings kit, use recycled objects to start seeds indoors. Old berry containers, toilet paper rolls, and empty yogurt cups can all make great places for seedlings to grow.

Did you know: Another way to grow new plants is by rooting them from a cutting. If you do this, invest in some rooting hormone, available at your local garden supply store. You just dip your cuttings into this powdery substance, and it really increases your chances of success.

18: Help Beautify Your Community

ADVENTURE SCALE: 3

The basics: Keeping the community beautiful is everyone's responsibility. Join a trash cleanup crew to keep waterways, beaches, campgrounds, and picnic areas clean. You don't have to wait for a special event, though. Always pick up trash you find in natural areas, even if it's not yours.

Challenge: Organize your own cleanup day. Local nonprofits love groups to come in and help out. Contact an organization near you, and spend a day helping them out.

Discover more: One of the easiest ways to get involved in beautifying your community is with the nonprofit Keep America Beautiful. Look on their website, kab.org, for information on how to get involved locally.

19: Celebrate International Migratory Bird Day

ADVENTURE SCALE: 2

The basics: International Migratory Bird Day (IMBD) is a day in May that celebrates birds around the world. Many nature centers, Audubon groups, and bird observatories plan special programs in honor of this day. It's a great opportunity to get outside and learn something new about the birds in your backyard.

Challenge: Attend a local bird walk. There are birding groups all over the country, and they'll often hold family bird walks. Find one to go on—you're sure to learn a lot. And don't worry about being an expert. The group will often supply binoculars for you to use, and no one expects you to know all the birds.

Discover more: You can get involved in this very cool event. Start by going to the website, birdday.org. Before you know it, you'll be making IMBD an annual tradition.

20: Bike to a Nearby Destination

ADVENTURE SCALE: 3

The basics: Biking is great exercise and fun, too. Instead of getting in a car for everything, try biking to a local park or playground instead. You might be surprised at how fast you get there and how much fun you have. Plus, bikes are often allowed in areas that cars aren't.

Challenge: Check out a local bike trail. Many communities have bike trails to get you around town. It's also a popular activity at many national parks and national wildlife refuges. So check one out near you.

Discover more: Go to your local bike shop. Often, they'll have free maps of routes to explore in your area. You might be surprised to find out just how many biking options you have.

21: Find Antlers in the Woods

ADVENTURE SCALE: 4

The basics: Male deer, elk, and moose all grow antlers to intimidate the other males and to impress the females. Covered in "velvet," these antlers can grow quickly and large, throughout the spring and summer. Since they are often shed in winter, spring is a great time to go antler hunting. It's illegal to collect antlers in certain areas, so check with wildlife officials before bringing them home.

Challenge: Find a complete pair. Antlers don't always fall off at the same time, so sometimes the right antler is miles away from the left one. If you can find a complete pair, that's even more rare.

Did you know: Caribou and reindeer are the same thing, and both male and female reindeer have antlers. So don't just assume a reindeer is a boy just because it has antlers.

22: Splash in a Puddle

ADVENTURE SCALE: 1

The basics: April showers don't just bring May flowers. They also bring instant smiles. Slip on your galoshes and take a rainy day walk. Splashing in the puddles will bring a smile to anyone's face. It's freeing to let yourself get a little wet and muddy.

Challenge: Everyone sings in the shower, but now it's time to get out and sing in the rain. Make sure there's no thunder and lightning, but then go outside and belt out a tune. Umbrellas are optional! It's fun to get wet (though you might want to have a warm shower or bath waiting for you when you're done).

Did you know: Deeper and bigger doesn't necessarily equal better splashes when it comes to puddles. For best results, go along the edges of puddles and stomp in the more shallow spots.

NATURE BINGO

Nature Bingo is just like regular Bingo, except instead of numbers, you have a board filled with nature objects. It's a good way to make a nature hike even more fun and interesting. You can also take it on the road, especially if you're going to be driving in the country at all. You can have a game of Nature Bingo right outside your window.

Ages: 4 and up
Materials: Cereal boxes, stickers or magazine cutouts, markers, glue
Length: 10 minutes or more
Number of players: 2 or more

1. First you need to create some Bingo cards. This is easy enough to do. Recycle old cereal boxes (or use any other cardboard) to make your own. To start, cut out 4 equal squares, roughly 6 inches by 6 inches. If you're going to have more than 4 players regularly, cut out more.
2. With the squares, draw a grid of 4 spaces across and 4 spaces down. You can put the name of your game, "NATURE BINGO," across the top. Then fill in the squares with nature items—use stickers, magazine cutouts, or draw your own pictures of items you find in nature. Be sure to have a mix of easy, medium, and hard things to find. Good examples include a bird, an orange flower, a frog, a large rock, a ladybug, a pine tree, and a birdhouse.
3. Remember, no 2 Bingo cards are alike. So when you draw or glue the items onto the cards, be sure to mix them up. This way, it's luck of the draw on who will bingo first.
4. Now go exploring. Every time you see something on your Bingo card, mark it off. The first one to get a straight line horizontal, vertical, or diagonal is the winner.

Tip

You can create several different Nature Bingo themes. Make it a project for the entire family. For example, put together a bird bingo, flower bingo, or leaf bingo. It's a good way to learn more about a specific thing in nature.

23: Tap a Maple Tree

ADVENTURE SCALE: 4

The basics: Maple trees are abundant throughout much of the country. As the weather warms, it's time to collect the sap. It's best to find someone who has the equipment and knowledge to do this properly, so look for a nature center near you offering this as a class or experience. It's an experience you won't forget.

Challenge: Make your own maple syrup. Again, it's best to find instructions for doing this properly. Or go to a syrup making class. Things always taste better when you know you made it yourself.

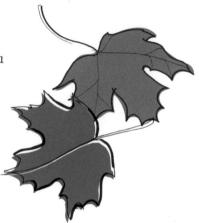

Did you know: You can tap all maple trees for sap, but sugar maples are traditionally thought of as the best. This sap has higher sugar content and produces more flavor. If you don't make your own syrup, consider buying syrup from an individual to support her local business.

24: Dig Clams

ADVENTURE SCALE: 4

The basics: Many people like to dig clams and eat them, but you don't have to like the taste of clams to enjoy digging for them. Wear your boots, bring a shovel, and prepare to get muddy. You can often dig clams from the mud exposed during a low tide. And if you're in an area where a shellfish license is required, be sure to get one.

Challenge: It's a specific taste and some people think they're a little slimy, but be brave and give a clam a try. Who knows, maybe you'll end up loving them. Be sure all clams are properly prepared before eating them.

Did you know: Clams are living things, but they have no head, arms, or legs. Their shell is what protects them from predators.

☐ 25: Plant at Least Three Different Veggies

ADVENTURE SCALE: 3

The basics: Whether you like traditional leafy greens, root veggies like carrots, or more unique things like eggplant, try planting a couple of your favorites. Then throw in at least one thing that you haven't tried before.

Challenge: Plant heirloom veggies. These veggies are seed strains that date back decades. It's fun to explore heirlooms for their colors, flavors, and textures. Many garden centers are starting to carry heirlooms these days, so be on the lookout.

Did you know: Think of vegetables in two different ways—roots and shoots. Root veggies grow under the ground as a root. Shoot veggies shoot up. For example, carrots and radishes are both roots, and corn and tomatoes are shoots.

GARDEN PIZZA

It's time to break out of the mold of ordinary pepperoni and cheese pizza. Just take a little inspiration from the garden, and make your own healthy variety instead. When it comes to garden pizza, anything goes. You don't know if you'll like it until you try it, so dare to think outside of the box. Hit up the local farmers' market for ideas on fresh ingredients you can use now. Or go to the grocery store for inspiration from the fruits and veggies there. Once you have the spring version down, in summer try making garden pizza again to see what new ingredients from the garden are available. First things first, though—make the dough. After that, let your imagination be your guide.

DIY Pizza Dough Serving size: 8

3 cups all-purpose flour
1 package (25 ounces) active dry yeast
3 tablespoons olive oil
1 teaspoon salt
2 teaspoons sugar
1 cup warm water

Combine all ingredients in a bowl. Once they're mixed together, begin kneading the dough, either with your hands or with a rolling pin. It helps if your pin or hands are lightly covered in flour first to avoid sticking. Knead your dough for 5–10 minutes. Spread out onto your greased pizza pan. Top with your favorite pizza sauce, garden ingredients, and cheese.

Garden Pizza Ideas

Spinach Pizza Don't cringe just because spinach is in the name. Pieces of fresh spinach and cheese make a yummy (and healthy) alternative to the traditional cheese pizza. Layer pizza sauce, spinach, and cheese.

Tomato Mozzarella Pizza You can either buy fresh mozzarella or use the shredded mozzarella in bags. Then slice up thin layers of Roma tomatoes. Layer pizza sauce, tomatoes, and cheese.

Carrot Pizza Instead of using carrots with a traditional tomato sauce, try an alfredo sauce instead. Layer alfredo sauce, carrots, and your favorite cheese.

Pepper Pizza Try finding several different pepper varieties to put on your pizza, both for color and taste. Layer pizza sauce, peppers, and cheese.

Tips and Tricks

Try experimenting; add even more fresh ingredients on your pizza. Things like pineapple, lettuce, broccoli, and mango are all options. Nothing is off limits.

26: Inspect a Lizard

ADVENTURE SCALE: 4

The basics: There are dozens of lizard species north of Mexico and most are harmless to handle. (The Gila Monster and a handful of other species are poisonous, so if you're not sure, inspect from a distance.) After you check them out, be sure to return them where you found them.

Challenge: Find a horned toad. A handful of horned lizard species go by the nickname of horny toad. These lizards have spines coming out of their heads and squat round bodies. They are especially common in the Southwest.

Did you know: Lizards and salamanders are the same, right? No way! They're very different, but here's one of the basics—lizards tend to have dry, scaly skins like snakes. Salamanders range from a bit moist to downright slimy.

27: Go to a Petting Zoo

ADVENTURE SCALE: 2

The basics: Local farms often put together petting zoos featuring friendly farm animals like chickens, goats, ponies, and pot-bellied pigs. This is an easy way to experience farm life up close. Look for a petting zoo at a festival, neighborhood party, or farm near you.

Challenge: Feed the animals from your hand. The people running the petting zoo will often have food you can buy or use. Sit back and let the animals come to you. Don't be scared. Just hold still, and you'll make a new friend.

Did you know: Don't just think the fuzzy little animals are the best at a petting zoo. Pot-bellied pigs and goats are some of the friendliest around.

28: See a Rainbow

ADVENTURE SCALE: 2

The basics: Rainbows often form after a light spring rain. They can even start to appear when it's still sprinkling a bit. So put on your raincoat and get outside for a rainbow hunt, because as soon as the rain fizzles out, you'll want to be ready.

Challenge: Find a double rainbow. They aren't very common, but it's a good challenge. Once you find one, take lots of pictures because you never know when another one will come along.

Did you know: You can't actually get to the end of a rainbow, so don't even try. When you move, the rainbow shifts with you. So you better leave discovering the end of a rainbow up to the fairytales.

29: Find Animal Tracks

ADVENTURE SCALE: 3

The basics: As snow melts away and spring showers fall, it can get a little sloppy outside. These conditions are ideal for finding animal tracks. Follow an animal trail through the meadow, or seek out tracks near water. Based on the tracks, see if you can find any clues about what the animal was doing.

Challenge: It's simple to make plaster casts out of animal tracks. You just need some plaster and a container to stir it up. Deep tracks, dried in mud, are the best impressions to capture in plaster. Start with a good plaster mix, available at craft stores. Next, pour the plaster in the track and then just let it dry.

Discover more: If you really want to ID tracks, pick up an animal tracks book at your local library or bookstore. Also check out the array of nature guides at Falcon.com. Once you study up a bit, you'll be able to identify tracks right away.

FAMILY FARMS

If you're lucky enough to live on a farm, then you already know about the great adventures you can find there every single day. But for most people, the most they know about farms comes from a song involving Old MacDonald. Don't let your farm experience be limited to "E-I-E-I-O."

Who? If you have both young and old in your family, then this is the place for you. Little ones will love petting or just looking at the animals and hearing all the sounds of the farm. Older kids can feed the animals, ride horses, and maybe even milk some cows.

What? A farm is always filled with activity, but it varies depending on what kind of farm it is. With family farms, you'll probably find a handful of animals to visit, a garden, and other activities. If you have a farm in your area that has regular business hours, call ahead to get an idea of what you can find there.

When? If you visit in spring, chances are you'll get to see lots of new life— new fields being planted, ducklings, chicks, and other baby animals. In fall, it's harvest time with pumpkins, apples, and more. Do a little checking with the family farms in your area to see if there are any special events planned.

Where? You might be surprised to find out about a family farm location. Even if you live in the city, it's probably a short drive to a local farm. Or if you live in a more rural area, you might have a few more options to choose from. Also, don't overlook all types of farms—pumpkin farms, dairy farms, horse farms—they're all great places to visit.

Why? Getting a taste of farm life is definitely worth your time. It helps you relax, take a step back, and realize where a lot of your food comes from. It's also a great way to see animals. So take a moment out of your busy schedule and relax on a farm.

Look around your area to find a farm to visit yourself. Some farms are open to the public already during certain hours. Otherwise, make friends with a local farmer. It's definitely worth the effort, and chances are, they'd love to show you the ropes.

30: Dig Your Own Worms for Fishing

ADVENTURE SCALE: 3

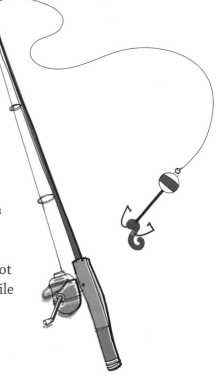

The basics: A couple of shovels of dirt can yield enough worms for an entire day of fishing. Pretty much all fish can be coaxed with worms, including trout, sunfish, bass, walleye, and catfish. For best results, dig for worms right after a spring rain.

Challenge: Catch grasshoppers for fishing instead. Grasshoppers are especially popular for bait on western trout streams. Watching a fish slurp up the grasshopper as it floats on top of the water is fun.

Did you know: Night crawlers are the most common worms sold for fishing, but that's not all you can use. If you find another worm while digging, give it a try. You never know what'll work.

31: Learn How to Skip Rocks

ADVENTURE SCALE: 4

The basics: A flat rock with straight edges skips the best. If your rock is too thin, it'll flutter off target, and if it's too thick, it'll plunk right to the bottom. Don't give up if you don't catch on right away. The trick is the flick of the wrist, so keep practicing.

Challenge: Have a contest to see who can get in the most skips. You could have five rounds total, and tally up all the skips together. This is a friendly competition anyone can join. If you practice enough, you can get really good.

Bonus video: Yes, it does take a little bit of technique and practice, but there are a few additional secrets that will help you skip rocks. Learn more at destinationnature.net.

32: Fly a Kite

ADVENTURE SCALE: 3

The basics: Pick a slightly breezy day, and go fly a kite. Be sure to fly your kite in an open area, clear of power lines and tree branches. A beach is an ideal setting with the refreshing water breeze keeping your kite soaring.

Challenge: After you master flying a kite, you can also learn to do kite tricks. Make your kite twist and dive. Some kites are especially designed to dart and jump through the sky. Look for kite shops where you can pick up a unique or interesting kite.

Discover more: April is National Kite Month. It's a great excuse to get outside and try flying kites. Learn more at nationalkitemonth.org.

33: Make Mud Pies

ADVENTURE SCALE: 2

The basics: The trick to a good mud pie is finding mud that isn't too wet or too dry. Scoop up a handful of mud, then paddy cake it flat. Craft it into a round shape, and serve up your mud pie to your friends. If it looks really good, you better remind them not to eat it.

Challenge: Can you be artsy with mud? Sure you can. Don't just stop at pies. With a little imagination, you can make a whole gourmet meal with mud. (Better ask mom first before you borrow any dishes from the kitchen.)

Discover more: There are actually real mud pies, not made from dirt. Mud pie recipes involve lots of chocolate and are a traditional southern dessert. Look online for a great recipe.

34: Make Sugar Water
ADVENTURE SCALE: 2

The basics: Spring is the time orioles and hummingbirds start coming around, so invest in a sugar-water feeder and attract these colorful birds. Sugar water is four parts water to one part sugar. Boil until it all dissolves. Let cool and fill feeders. Be sure to change out the water every few days so it stays fresh.

Challenge: Put up a hanging basket near your feeder. This will give hummingbirds an extra source of nectar, and it creates a more natural setting. This will increase your chance of success in attracting these cool birds.

Did you know: A lot of people think you have to add red food coloring to sugar water to attract hummingbirds, but that's not the case at all. In fact, it's best to leave it plain, which means fewer steps overall.

35: Pack a Picnic Lunch
ADVENTURE SCALE: 2

The basics: It only takes a little bit of planning to organize a picnic lunch. Plan items that won't get smashed and are easy to eat without utensils. Then pack the food away in a picnic basket or a backpack. Then use it as an excuse to go someplace fun and enjoy lunch amid nature. Don't forget water.

Challenge: Have an adventurous lunch by going on a difficult hike or kayaking trip. Then you can have your lunch once you get to your destination. What a great way to celebrate your accomplishment!

Did you know: National Picnic Day is always held in April, during Earth Month. Look up events near you so you can be a part of it. Then solicit family friends or neighbors. You could have a ginormous picnic.

SALADS

Spring is the ideal time to grow lettuce in the backyard. Whether you grow your own or pick up this tasty and nutritious green from your local farmers' market, use the season as an excuse to experiment with salads. Here are a couple of classic recipes to try, but feel free to branch out and create your own.

Strawberry Spinach Salad Serving size: 4

4-5 cups spinach

2 cups fresh strawberries, sliced

1/2 cup sliced almonds

1/4 cup blue cheese crumbles

Raspberry or strawberry vinaigrette

Mix in the first four ingredients. When you're ready to serve it, mix in a few tablespoons of dressing. (Don't worry about spending the time to make your own dressing. There are great berry vinaigrettes at the store.) Toss gently. If the salad is too dry, you can add in a little bit more dressing, but don't overdo it. You don't need a lot.

Cobb Salad Serving size: 4

5-6 cups lettuce

Sliced avocado

Sliced olives

Bacon bits

Cooked, sliced egg

Chopped tomatoes

Your favorite cheese

Cubed chicken or ham (optional)

Wash and tear your lettuce into small pieces. Place on the bottom of a bowl. Layer the rest of the ingredients in rows, one right after the other. Skip what you don't like, but keep the layers going to create a pretty display. If you'd like, you can add cooked, cubed chicken or ham. Once everything is in place, top with your favorite dressing. Many cobb salads are traditionally served with ranch, but have fun and mix it up however you like it.

Tips and Tricks

You can put just about anything on a salad. For other fruits, try adding apples, mango, pineapple, and mandarin oranges. For veggies, pretty much anything tastes good, so pile it on. Then try mixing your own dressings using a seasoning packet you pick up at the grocery store. You'll get a fresh, tasty flavor—much better than a lot of bottled dressings.

36: Find a Moss-Covered Log

ADVENTURE SCALE: 3

The basics: Moss thrives in cool, damp places. And it's really soft and gentle to the touch. Go on a little moss hunt in some woods or shaded spots in your area. Notice the moss—where it's growing, how much of it there is, what color it is, and so on.

Challenge: Discover a moss bed for yourself. Find a fallen tree or log that is wider than your shoulders. Then crawl on top, and take a little snooze on your natural bed.

Did you know: Moss doesn't have a root system, so it can grow just about anywhere, from the ground to rocks and logs. You can also find it growing on a tree trunk. It likes moist conditions, so look for it in shady or damp areas.

37: Go Sailing

ADVENTURE SCALE: 4

The basics: Sailing isn't just for the ocean, and you don't have to have a sailboat to try it out. Many people sail on large inland lakes too. Find a local sailing club in your area or see if you can take lessons from someone you know. You have to try it at least once.

Challenge: Make your own sailboat out of sticks, leaves, or other natural materials. It is fun to see what you can make float. How long will your boat float?

Did you know: A boat race is called a regatta. Sailing is a long-standing Olympic sport that used to be known as yachting. The races can be a lot of fun to watch.

38: Listen to a Waterfall

ADVENTURE SCALE: 3

The basics: Every waterfall has a unique sound. The water cascading down can be a soothing trickle or a nearly unbearable thunder. Find a secure place to take in the sounds. Then close your eyes and simply listen.

Challenge: While many waterfalls are easy to get to, some of the most beautiful require a bit more effort. Hiking to a waterfall will make you appreciate the experience even more. Take a camera, so you can get lots of great pictures.

Discover more: If you love waterfalls and like to visit them when you travel, then you have to check out the World Waterfall Database, worldwaterfalldatabase.com. You can find cool waterfalls all over the world on this site.

39: Look Closely at a Spider Web

ADVENTURE SCALE: 2

The basics: Spiders are some of nature's true engineers. Their web silk is some of the strongest material in the world. Study the construction of spider webs closely. What is the web attached to? Is the web simple or complex in design?

Challenge: Look at a spider under a microscope or magnifying glass to examine its distinctive anatomy. When you get an up-close look at spiders, you'll see that they're not scary at all and are really pretty cool.

Did you know: Spiders are not insects. They are in a family all on their own. The biggest difference between spiders and other insects is spiders only have two main body parts while other insects have three.

VINTAGE BIRDHOUSES

Want to create a unique, interesting birdhouse for the birds in your backyard? Now you can, using an album cover from an old vinyl record. The whole project shouldn't cost more than $5–$10 and maybe even less if you already have some of the supplies at home. It's a great gift, especially for someone who likes music and the birds.

Supplies: Birdhouse, vinyl album covers, paper, scissors, glue, string, two screws, outdoor sealer
Ages: Any age, though younger kids might need a little help
Time: 20 minutes

How-To:

1. First things first—you need a birdhouse. If you already have one at home that you want to redo, just clean it up a bit and it should be fine to use. If you don't have a birdhouse at home, check out your local nature store or even craft store. You just need a basic design. Don't spend extra money on anything fancy. Most craft stores have a wood section, and you can pick up a pre-built birdhouse for less than $5.
2. This is the fun part. Go to a local rummage sale or thrift store to look for old vinyl albums. You can usually pick them up for less than $1. There might even be some old albums in your attic. Look for colorful ones that have fun designs. Also, look for ones that you can cut in many different ways so they'll still look unique.
3. Once you have your birdhouse and vinyl albums, use a piece of paper to trace all the sides (and roof) of the birdhouse. These will be your patterns for cutting out the album cover, so try to make it as exact as possible. You'll need to make as many patterns as you have different shapes.
4. Use your new patterns to then trace the cardboard album covers you have. Be sure to position the patterns so you're cutting out interesting and/or colorful sections of the album.
5. Cut out the shapes.

6. Glue the shapes onto the birdhouse using a strong glue like Mod Podge from a craft store.
7. After letting it dry, add screws to the top in the front and back of the birdhouse. Tie a string to the screws so the birdhouse has something to hang from.
8. Spray with a sealer especially made to withstand the outdoors. Hang up your newly decorated birdhouse and wait for the birds to come make it home.

Tips and Tricks

When you choose a birdhouse, make sure the entry hole isn't too big (most only require about an inch or two). If it is too big, it might invite predators in or attract squirrels. Also, there doesn't need to be a perch.

Bonus Video

Want to see how this is done? Get a closer look at our how-to video on making a birdhouse out of old record covers available at destinationnature.net.

40: Find Your State Bird

ADVENTURE SCALE: 3

The basics: Every state has a state bird. Which species represents your state? Once you find out, grab a pair of binoculars and get out there to find it!

Challenge: The bald eagle is our national symbol, so go out and see if you can spot one of these magnificent fliers. If you like eagles, you might also go online to check out some of the famous eagle cams where you can watch the eagles raise their young.

Did you know: If you're looking for your state bird (or flower, tree, and more for that matter), go to 50states.com. This is a great website with lots of good information divided by state.

41: Catch a Dragonfly

ADVENTURE SCALE: 3

The basics: Dragonflies often patrol the edge of water or open meadows. They are agile fliers and can be difficult to catch in a net. If you manage to scoop one up, gently hold the wings back and look at it closely. After a few minutes, be sure to release it.

Challenge: Find a damselfly. Damselflies are closely related to dragonflies. You'll recognize them because they hold their wings behind them when they are perched.

Did you know: Huge, dinosaur-like dragonflies used to exist. There are fossil records of one dragonfly that had a wingspan of more than two feet.

42: Swing on a Tire Swing

ADVENTURE SCALE: 3

The basics: If you know of someone that has a tire swing in your area, ask him if you can give it a try. If not, consider hanging one of your own in the backyard. You just need a sturdy branch, some rope, and an old tire.

Challenge: What's more fun than a tire swing? Try a rope swing! Many campgrounds have rope swings, and you can fly through the air into a pond. Or try climbing the rope swing all the way to the top.

Did you know: You can turn a tire swing either vertical or horizontal. If you turn it flat, you can fit a couple of people on it at a time. Check out playgrounds in your area to see how they hang their tire swings. It'll give you good tips for how to do yours.

❏ 43: Catch a Crawdad
ADVENTURE SCALE: 4

The basics: Also called crawfish or crayfish, crawdads are fresh water creatures that you can often find in shallow areas. (They are closely related to lobsters.) Be careful when you're trying to catch one—they do have little pinchers.

Challenge: Devise a crawdad trap. If you want to catch a few dozen crawdads (some people like to eat them), you're going to need a trap. Look online for specifications for building your own, or buy one instead.

Did you know: There's a reason the South is known for crawfish. They have more species there than anywhere. Crawfish rely on clean water to survive and thrive.

❏ 44: Cook Hot Dogs over a Campfire
ADVENTURE SCALE: 2

The basics: Hot dogs always seem to taste better when you cook them over an open fire. Grab a pack, make your skewers out of sticks, and roast some up. You can roast hot dogs any time of the year, but the first hot dogs of spring always seem to taste a little bit better.

Challenge: Make your entire meal over the fire. This might take a little more equipment than a stick or two, but it's a good challenge. You can even roast veggies on your skewer. Be patient—it might take a while.

Discover more: You can find entire cookbooks dedicated to cooking over a fire. *Over a Fire* is one option and *Cooking on a Stick* is another. Also, look in the cookbook section of your library for other similar books.

45: Identify Constellations

ADVENTURE SCALE: 3

The basics: Sometimes you have to take a minute and just watch the world around you. Go outside at night. You might want to take a few blankets because it might be chilly out. Then look up at the stars and see if you can spot some of the most common constellations, like the Big Dipper or Orion.

Challenge: Don't stop at just one or two—find more constellations. Check out a book about stars from your local library, and then look for some of those lesser-known groupings. They are just as much fun to find as the bigger ones.

Discover more: For those of you who really love astronomy, visit the website kidsastronomy.com. It has lots of great information and games.

46: Find a Turtle

ADVENTURE SCALE: 2

The basics: Some turtles like to hang out near the water while you can find others in the woods. Most turtles are easy to handle, and you can take a close look at them. But watch out for snapping turtles—you'll want to keep your distance.

Challenge: Spot a turtle with its young. You can often find young turtles lined up on a log near the water. They can be hard to spot—they often camouflage themselves against the park—but once you spot them, they're hard to miss.

Did you know: What's the difference between a tortoise and a turtle? Both are reptiles, but there are many other differences. For instance, turtles have webbed feet while tortoise feet are short and sturdy. Tortoises also have heavier shells while turtle shells are more lightweight.

DUCK, DUCK, GOOSE

Ages: 3 and up
Materials: None
Length: 15 minutes
Number of players: 5 or more

Duck, Duck, Goose is one of the most classic childhood games of all time. Anyone can play, young and old alike. You just need to be able to run. In Duck, Duck, Goose, there's no exact winner per se, but it's a fun way to get an entire group up and moving.

1. The bigger the group the better with Duck, Duck, Goose. So gather up as many friends as you can. Then have them all sit in a giant circle. One person is chosen to be "it." He is the designated goose for now.
2. The goose walks around the circle, gently tapping people on the head as he passes. As the goose taps them, he chants "duck, duck, duck, duck." Once this person is ready to choose someone else to be it, he will tap the person on the head and declare "goose!"
3. The goose jumps up and chases the person who was it, trying to tag him. The original goose has to run all around the circle and try to get back into the spot of the person tagged before that person catches up to him.
4. If the new goose reaches the original goose before he takes his spot, that person has to go into the middle of the circle. Then he has to stay there until another person gets caught and has to go in the middle.
5. The new goose goes around the circle again and the game continues.

Tip
Duck, Duck, Goose doesn't have a lot of rules, but here's a good one to enforce if you can. Make it a rule that you have to choose a new person each time. This way, everyone will get a turn, and you won't get people picking the same ones over and over again.

Did You Know?
In some areas of the country, the game is called Duck, Duck, Gray Duck instead.

47: Create a Fort

ADVENTURE SCALE: 5

The basics: A fort can be as small or as big as you want. You can create one in the woods or just out in your own backyard. Have fun with it—create secret rules, make a sign, and invite your friends to join. You can even buy garden frames where you can grow your own fort! The plants will grow up the frame creating walls.

Challenge: Create a tree house. This is a lot more work, and you'll probably need someone to help. But a tree house will offer up fun for years. If it's out of the question to have your own, try to find a tree house that you can visit. Perhaps a local park or botanical garden has one built.

Bonus video: Want to know one of the easiest ways to build a fort? Visit destinationnature.net for a video that gives you an easy fort solution you can make in less than 10 minutes.

48: Build a Sandcastle

ADVENTURE SCALE: 3

The basics: You need some buckets, a good sand shovel, and a few good sculpting tools for added details. Be sure to find good packing sand—you might have to dig a little to find sand that is a little bit wet so it holds together better. Start the castle small with a couple of towers, and then solicit some help from friends to grow it bigger.

Challenge: Create a sand village. You can make several homes, a river, a moat, and more. Then if you'd like, you can even add people, cars, and other toys to make it into a big game.

Did you know: Around beach communities, you can often find sandcastle competitions, which are fascinating to watch. Look for one to attend if you live near the beach or plan to go on vacation when one of these takes place.

49: Watch a Bird-Banding Demonstration

ADVENTURE SCALE: 3

The basics: Bird banding is popular in spring. It's a good time for researchers to track bird migration, so they use bands to help them learn more about birds in the area. Find a banding demo at a nature center, bird observatory, or Audubon center in your area. Be sure to take your camera—it might be your best chance to get a close picture of a bird.

Challenge: Touch a bird. Only trained banders generally handle a bird, but they might let you touch its feathers or even help let it go. It's cool to feel how soft and gentle the feathers are.

Discover more: There are more than a million birds banded every year, and you have to hold a special permit in order to do it. If you see or find a banded bird, help researchers by reporting it to reportband.gov.

50: Find Spring Snow

ADVENTURE SCALE: 4

The basics: Winter likes to linger in northern and mountainous regions. You can also find bits of snow in heavily shaded areas where it stays cool. Go on a hike and see if you can find a little bit of snow in your area. Chances are, it's been there for months.

Challenge: Find watermelon snow. First of all, you need to know what it is. Also called snow algae or red snow, watermelon snow is caused by a type of algae and often shows up in spring. But don't eat it, or you'll get sick.

Did you know: Snow in Hawaii? It's true. Nearly all mountains (if you go high enough) have snow. So while most people go to Hawaii for the sun and beaches, you could also go to ski.

NATURE CENTERS

Nature centers can be great places to explore during the spring. Reptiles and amphibians are reemerging from their winter stupor. Migratory birds return in waves. And tree buds start to pop, so there's something to see wherever you go.

Who? Nature centers can be good for a short visit, or can offer a place to explore day after day all year long. They'll have activities and learning opportunities for all ages. Nature tot programs are growing in popularity for the youngest of explorers. Or ask about starting up a family nature club or a young birders club at your local nature center. Nature centers often do programs for schools, scouts, and civic groups. Some even host birthday parties!

What? A nature center can be a grand place to explore on your own or with a professional naturalist guide. Many will have interpretive trails to help you understand what you see around you. Be sure to check out the inside of the center for a chance to explore touch tables, see displays, and learn about upcoming events. Get up close to nature while exploring the bird feeding stations or butterfly gardens.

When? Take advantage of the longer days and the warmer temperatures to explore outside. Some nature centers will have shorter trails while others will have an extensive network of trails suitable for all-day excursions. Many are open sunrise to sunset, and some will offer special night hike events and owl prowls.

Where? Nature centers can be operated by any number of organizations, but the one thing they all have in common is they are outstanding places to go for nature adventures. Many are free, while some require a small entrance fee, trail fee, or program fees. Family memberships can often get you year-round access to these wonderful facilities.

Why? Nature centers are perfect because they highlight the local plants and animals that you'll be able to find in your own backyard. They'll have tons of hands-on learning experiences for everyone.

Tips and Tricks
Bird observatories are similar to nature centers, but they have an added focus on researching birds. Many bird observatories offer educational programs and bird banding demonstrations, and some host International Migratory Bird Day celebrations each May. If you have a special interest in birds, look into this great resource. You can also consider volunteering. They'll have something you can do to help out.

SUMMER

*"I wonder what it would be like to live in a world
where it was always June."*

—L. M. MONTGOMERY

Summer is definitely the best season. Think about it—it's the ultimate
season for fun in the sun. The dog days of summer are great for adventure, whether simply relaxing in the backyard or taking road trips across
the country.

Perhaps one of the greatest things about summer is the clothes. Now is
the time to bust out the flip-flops and shorts. Or hit the lake for a little bit of
excitement. The water will be refreshing, whether you're swimming or fishing.

The summer sun keeps the temperature warm. Even when it's hot,
remember that all the vibrant sunshine helps nourish the garden. You can
stay busy all season long planting, watering, weeding, harvesting, and
eating what you've grown. Or, if you like to
stick to flowers, planting your backyard
landscape can provide habitat for numerous
critters, including birds and butterflies.

Tadpoles and sunning snakes welcome
the summer season. Butterflies, moths,
dragonflies, and fireflies keep bug watchers happy day and night all summer long.
Many mammals are crepuscular, most
active at dawn and dusk, especially during
the hot summer months. Meanwhile,
fledgling birds are learning how to fly,
a truly entertaining sight.

If you venture out beyond town, you'll be rewarded with stars and perhaps a glimpse of the Milky Way at night. State and national parks are great options, and while they are popular destinations for many, you can still go beyond the basic trailheads to have the whole place to yourself.

Summer has the longest days of the year. How will you celebrate this bonus daylight? Maybe you want to turn your family reunion into a nature adventure this summer. Go ahead and gather up your brothers, sisters, and cousins, and pick teams for summer games. It doesn't matter what you like to do; this is the season to get things done.

Summer adventure awaits. Just open the door, step outside, and let the fun begin.

Summer's Checklist

☐ 1: Jump in the Middle of the Lake

ADVENTURE SCALE: 4

The basics: It can be scary to jump in water and swim when your feet don't touch, but face your fears and take the leap. Go out to the middle of the lake in a boat or canoe, and jump. Of course, always wear a life jacket, especially if you're not a strong swimmer.

Challenge: Do a cannonball in the middle of the lake. Challenge your friends, and see who can make the biggest splash.

Did you know: You know how they say wildlife is more scared of us than we are of them? It's true, and it's no different than with fish. Think about it—if something huge splashes into the water around you, wouldn't you swim away?

☐ 2: Pitch a Tent

ADVENTURE SCALE: 4

The basics: It's harder than you think, but it's a little bit like riding a bike. Once you get the hang of it, it's pretty easy. Follow the instructions carefully, and make sure you secure your tent at the corners. You don't want all that hard work to be ruined by a big gust of wind.

Challenge: Get one of those huge tents with multiple compartments. They're a challenge to set up, but once you do, they're so cool. You can have a whole party inside.

Discover more: If you love camping, be sure to check out gocamping america.com. It has plenty of camping destinations to keep you busy for years.

LAKES

Lakes are one of the hottest spots to be in summer. No matter where you live, there's probably a lake within driving distance. You might not even know it existed. Make sure it's not a private lake, and then make plans to go for the day. Lakes are also the perfect place to take your boat, canoe, and kayak.

Who? Everyone can go to the lake, but the ages of those going will determine what you need to bring. Babies will probably need something to ride in if they're going in the water. Older kids will probably want to bring water toys or even skis or a tube to pull behind a boat. Remember that if you go on a boat of any sort, you'll need life jackets for everyone. So bring those along unless your area lake has a public beach area where you can rent them.

What? Lakes vary a great deal as to what's offered, so do a little research before you go. Some have campsites and entertainment areas with games, water toys, food, and more. You can even rent boats or pontoons at some locations. Even private lakes could still have public access areas. You can spend a whole day fishing, boating, doing water games, or just relaxing.

When? The best time to go to the lake is when it's hot, and the water is cool and refreshing. If you live in northern areas, you might want to wait until later in the summer to go to the lake because it'll take a while for the water to warm up. Or if you live in a hot area, you might want to go earlier before the water gets too hot! Either way, sunny days are the best. Don't forget the sunblock!

Where? This is where it varies quite a bit by where you live. There are areas that have huge natural lakes that go on for miles and miles. Other areas have much smaller lakes, but they're everywhere. Go online and do a search for lakes in your area. Chances are, you have one by you. And don't worry if you don't have a boat. There are still plenty of things to do.

Why? Lakes are often near forests or other natural areas that you wouldn't otherwise discover. It's a great excuse to get outside and go swimming or fishing. And because lakes often have campsites nearby, those are two good experiences to combine.

Tips and Tricks
You don't have to have a boat to enjoy a day at the lake. Just pack up your swimsuits, lunch, a cooler, and some fishing gear, and you'll have plenty to keep you busy. And don't overlook rivers. You can have a lot of fun along the river, enjoying many of the same activities as on a lake.

BONUS VIDEO
Get tips for getting in and out of a kayak without tipping it over, at destinationnature.net.

❏ 3: Catch a Firefly

ADVENTURE SCALE: 2

The basics: Get a jar ready and poke air holes in the top. Then catch and fill your jar with fireflies at night. Take a close look at their bodies and where the glow comes from. And watch how they glow differently. They can actually communicate with each other through glowing.

Challenge: Crickets are also out at night, but they're hard to find. Challenge yourself to find one and catch it. Make sure you let both the crickets and fireflies go after a little while.

Did you know: Female fireflies will sometimes eat male fireflies. It sounds weird, but it's true. This isn't the case for all species, but still—it's a pretty impressive fact to share with your friends.

❏ 4: Play Catch

ADVENTURE SCALE: 3

The basics: The simple joy of playing catch never gets old. Either break out a baseball and a couple of mitts with a friend or get any other kind of ball to throw or kick back and forth. Go outside and enjoy the fresh air of your own backyard or a local park.

Challenge: See how many times you can throw a ball back and forth without dropping it. If you don't have a ball, just blow up a balloon and see how long you can keep it off the ground. What's the longest streak you can go?

Discover more: If you like baseball, check out a major or minor league team near you. They will often have kid days where they let kids run around the bases. It's an experience you'll always remember.

5: Plant a Second Garden

ADVENTURE SCALE: 3

The basics: It might seem a little early to be thinking about starting a second garden when your tomatoes and peppers are still growing, but it's not. Plant a second crop of carrots, and get your pumpkin seeds in the ground so you can have jack-o-lanterns for Halloween (see our Four-Season Garden project on page 18).

Challenge: Grow gourds. These are good for fall. Then you can dry them and turn them into birdhouses. You can find some pretty unusual gourd shapes out there, so look hard to find some seeds to grow something unique.

Did you know: Lettuce is also a good second crop to plant. Lettuce likes cooler weather, so wait until later in the summer so it can grow into fall as well. If the weather starts to get too cold, you can always cover the plants and protect them.

6: Find a Young Bird

ADVENTURE SCALE: 3

The basics: Summer is a great time to spot young birds. You might see them up in trees or on the ground, chirping and hoping that their parents will keep feeding them. They don't look like adult birds—their markings might be a little different. So keep an eye out.

Challenge: It's going to be difficult, but see if you can watch a young bird learn how to fly. Observing a nest daily will help increase your chance of seeing that first flight. Look up how long a particular bird species stays in the nest; then you'll have a better idea of when the birds might fly.

Did you know: One of the easiest young birds to spot is the American robin. They almost look like full-grown robins at first glance, and they are as big. But juveniles have spots on their breasts, making them easy to pick out. You can find them hanging out on the ground in mid- to late summer.

CONTAINER GARDENING

Container gardening is a quick and easy way to get growing. Anyone can have containers; whether you live in a house, apartment, or condo, you can always find a spot to tuck a container with a few plants. Here are the top things to remember when growing containers.

Get a good soil mix. You can't just use the soil in your backyard. Invest in a good potting mix, specifically designed for containers. It'll pay off.

Don't forget to water. Many container plants don't make it because they don't get enough water. Plants in containers need more water than usual. Let your sense of touch be your guide—if the soil feels dry, it's time to water.

Less is more. Don't overfill the container. A few plants can go a long way. It might look bare in the beginning, but it won't take long to fill in.

Mix it up. At the least, you'll want more of a tall plant with a trailing one. Read the plant labels first. Plant second.

Plan your plants ahead of time. Some plants need sun. Some like shade. Do a little research first, and then go in with a plan so you know which plants to pair together.

Get inspiration from your garden center. They have containers there, ready to buy as is. Buy one of these or at least look at what's in them. They'll provide a good guide for what you should be buying.

Learn the magic of succulents. Succulents do great in containers—they don't require as much water, and they'll grow almost anywhere. Hens and chicks is one option, but there are several others, too. Succulents are especially great if you have a shallow container because they don't need a huge space for the roots.

Save money. If you're looking to save money on your containers, consider growing some plants from seed. For example, zinnias are good ones to grow that will do great in containers. Start the seeds inside first and then plant the seedlings directly into the containers.

1. **The traditional route.** Find a pot. There are hundreds to choose from. Place your container where you want it first (in case it gets too heavy to move), then fill with soil and your plants.

2. **Hanging baskets.** Again, there are many options on the market. If you have the space, try a design. For instance, alternating pinks and purples along the eaves of a house would look gorgeous.

3. **Unique containers.** Here anything goes. Look for baskets, old pans, or anything else you can find to turn into a container. Remember to give your plants space, so if you have a small item, only put in a few plants. And if you use a shallow item, like a shoe, use succulents.

Tips and Tricks

Most people grow annuals in containers and get new plants each year, but you can use perennials too. If you want your perennials to survive from one year to the next, be sure to protect them over winter, either by bringing them inside or covering them.

7: Harvest Honey

ADVENTURE SCALE: 5

The basics: Try to find a beekeeper in the area or look for a bee program at a nearby nature center. See if you can help process the honey that has already been gathered from the bees. It's cool to see the magic happen, and tasting fresh honey is so yummy.

Challenge: Help gather the honeycomb from the hive. You'll need to make sure you wear protective gear and work with a beekeeper that knows what he's doing, but it's an amazing experience.

Did you know: Have you heard of the term "queen bee"? Well, it really does relate back to bees. The queen bee is the one in the hive that is the dominant female. She's usually deep in the hive, protected. Her job is to lay eggs so there are more bees to keep working the hive.

8: Make a Wish on a Dandelion

ADVENTURE SCALE: 1

The basics: Wishing is fun, especially when you're outside in nature. Pick a fluffy dandelion, take a deep breath, and blow! Legend has it that if you can blow off every last piece of fluff, then your wish will come true.

Challenge: Find a flower, and do the classic game of "he loves me, he loves me not." Except this time, ask your flower a question like a Magic Eight Ball. Then pick the petals off one at a time—yes, no, yes, no, etc. Whatever the last petal is will be your answer.

Did you know: A lot of people really hate dandelions. They get in the way of perfectly manicured lawns. But they're actually edible, and birds will use them for nesting material. If you have any in your lawn, take notice to see if birds or other backyard critters visit them.

9: Try Outdoor Yoga

ADVENTURE SCALE: 3

The basics: You might think yoga is easy, but it's challenging. Try a few yoga poses on your own on a beach, at a park, or somewhere else in nature. Or look for an outdoor yoga class to try.

Challenge: Why stop at yoga? Look up a few tai chi moves to try while you're at it. These sports might seem a bit slow-moving for some, but it takes incredible balance and strength to do a lot of the moves right.

Did you know: Many professional athletes do yoga. It might be funny to imagine these big athletes trying out yoga poses, but it really helps to make them agile and flexible.

10: Find Mushrooms

ADVENTURE SCALE: 4

The basics: It's fun to go on a wild mushroom hunt. Find a mushroom guide to see if you can ID them. Many mushrooms are poisonous (they can even be deadly), so don't even think about taste-testing them unless you are 100 percent sure what they are.

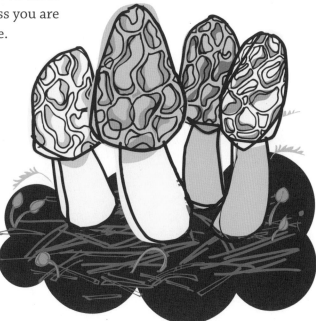

Challenge: Buy some mushrooms from a local farmers' market, and then use them in a dish. Challenge yourself to try something beyond the ordinary.

Did you know: Morel mushrooms are very difficult to find and are considered a delicacy. You can find entire groups or websites dedicated to hunting out these specific mushrooms.

KICKBALL

Kickball is a lot like baseball except anyone can play it, and you don't need a lot of equipment like bats or gloves. You just need a ball (the size of a basketball works well, but it should be softer and bouncier so you can easily kick it) and lots of players. This is one of the greatest things about this game—you can have 20 people or more. So gather up kids in the neighborhood or start up a friendly match at the family reunion. Keeping score is optional.

Ages: 4 and up
Materials: Ball
Length: 30 minutes to an hour
Number of players: 10 or more

1. Kickball follows most of the same rules as baseball, though you probably don't want to allow stealing. So to get started, set up the bases. You can use things like trees or bushes or make your own bases out of cardboard.
2. Next, choose teams and settle on some basic rules. Are you allowed to get people out by hitting them with the ball (it might depend on how hard of a ball you are using)? Are you playing three outs to an inning like traditional baseball? Will you have traditional strikes?
3. Once you have your rules set, team names set, and positions figured out, start playing. Remember, there are a few differences in kickball. For instance, the pitcher rolls the ball to the batters.
4. Cheering is encouraged! Keep in mind that this is a friendly game, but it's okay to do a little smack talking as long as it's all in good fun. If you do want to keep score, decide how many innings to play and then have someone be the official scorekeeper. You might have an impartial umpire keep score and be the one to call close plays.

Tips and Tricks

With kickball, you don't need a lot of space because the ball doesn't tend to go that far. Test out several different types of balls—you might find that it's more fun to play with a larger ball, but it's harder to handle.

11: Make a Sand Angel

ADVENTURE SCALE: 2

The basics: You've heard of a snow angel, right? Well now it's time to make an angel in the sand. Lie back and wave your arms and legs back and forth. Once you get up, look back to see your creation.

Challenge: Create sand art. You know the damp beach area near the water? Use a stick to create a masterpiece. See how intricate you can make the design before the tide comes in and washes it away.

Did you know: You can create other "angel" prints—just use your imagination. For instance, how about a grass angel on a fresh cut lawn? Or what about a leaf angel from a big pile of leaves in the fall?

12: Find Caterpillars

ADVENTURE SCALE: 3

The basics: The good thing about finding caterpillars is you know just where to look. They'll be on plant leaves, often the underside. Go to your garden or a nearby park and gently lift up the leaves. Remember, they might not be very big. Caterpillars start off very tiny.

Challenge: Find a monarch caterpillar. Monarch butterflies only lay their eggs on milkweed. So first find out what milkweed looks like, and then look for the yellow and black stripes of monarch caterpillars.

Did you know: Monarch Watch is a wonderful organization that is working to increase the monarch population across North America. Learn how you can help their efforts to increase the monarch population by going to monarchwatch.com. You can even track monarch migration online, which is cool to follow.

13: Collect Your Own Chicken Eggs
ADVENTURE SCALE: 2

The basics: Fresh farm eggs are yummy, and they're even better when you collect them yourself. If you don't have chickens yourself, find a local farm or egg supplier. Ask them if you could stop by sometime to visit the chickens and help collect the eggs. They'll probably be happy to show you around.

Challenge: Have you ever held a baby chick? They're so soft and fuzzy. Petting zoos might have baby chicks or ask a farm that has chickens. It's a great experience.

Discover more: Have you heard of CSAs? Community Supported Agriculture is when you can sign up to get a crop share from a farm. This can include everything from fruits and veggies to farm-fresh eggs. Learn how to sign up for a CSA by going to localharvest.org.

14: Take Flower Photos
ADVENTURE SCALE: 2

The basics: You don't have to have a fancy camera to get good flower pictures. Many plants hit their peak bloom time in summer, so have your camera ready. Lots of cameras even have a flower setting you can choose. Try all different angles and distances to get the best shot.

Challenge: Flowers are fairly easy photo subjects because they stay still. After you've mastered flowers, challenge yourself by trying to get a good photo of a bird or butterfly.

Did you know: Most digital cameras have a macro setting, and this is perfect for taking flower pictures or other close-ups. Try it out, and practice, practice, practice.

15: Find a Fox or a Bunny Hole

ADVENTURE SCALE: 3

The basics: Foxes and bunnies are both animals that use burrows. A burrow is just a fancy word for a home that is in the ground. You can often find foxes and bunnies around small hills, which are easy for them to dig out. Don't get too close, though. You still want to respect the burrow. It's an animal's home after all.

Challenge: This will take a little—no a lot—of patience, but see if you can spot a bunny or fox going in or out of that hole. You might have more luck spotting one early in the morning or later in the day just before it gets dark. Don't give up—they have to come back sooner or later.

Did you know: Desert tortoises, prairie dogs, and badgers are three other animals that live in holes. Can you do a little looking to see what others do as well?

16: Collect Your Own Herbs

ADVENTURE SCALE: 2

The basics: To collect your own herbs, you first need to plant them. So if you don't have herbs in your garden, you might want to add them. If you don't have your own, ask a friend if you can harvest some herbs from her. A little goes a long way with herbs. Chances are she'll have plenty to spare.

Challenge: Dry, save, and store your own herbs. Again, herb plants produce so much that you'll never be able to use them all fresh. Hang them upside down to dry them. Then grind them up and store them in little containers for future use. (You could even give these away as a gift.)

Discover more: Want to learn more about herbs and get the latest and greatest picks? The Herb Society of America is a great resource. Learn more at herbsociety.org.

MARBLE CHECKERS

Here's a simple project to turn some of your best nature photos into pieces for a checkerboard. Flowers and leaves make great art and are easy subjects to take photos of because they barely move. They'll make great checkers pieces—the leaves versus the flowers. After you have your photos selected, it's time to make the pieces. Here's how.

Supplies: Large clear marbles with flat sides, round hole punch, clear glue, construction paper
Ages: Kids 8 and up can do this project all by themselves, and 3–7 might need a little help from adults.
Time: The project itself only takes 15 to 20 minutes, but they'll need to dry overnight.

How-To:

1. First off, decide which photos to use for the checkers. If you don't have photos, use this as an excuse to get out in nature and take some. Have them printed at your local photo shop as wallet sizes. This will get them small enough to make a nice-size checker.
2. Use a round hole punch (about 3/4 inch or 1 inch) to punch your hole into the photo (and to punch out the photo in the round shape). When shopping at the craft store, look for your clear marbles and hole punch at the same time to make sure they will line up.
3. Place your photo face down on the flat side of the marble. (These marbles are available at local craft stores.) Then apply glue that dries to clear to the back of the photo. Press down hard to make sure you don't have any air bubbles. Repeat with your other marbles and photos.
4. Let the marbles dry overnight. To get a secure hold, you might even consider stacking a few heavy books on top.

5. The next day, clean off the front of the marbles and the excess dried glue. Then cover with a piece of construction paper so that the marbles have a smooth and colorful back.

6. They're ready to use. Get out a checkerboard and start a game. If you don't have a checkerboard, consider making your own out of a large piece of cardboard. This is a fun side project, and then you can decorate it any way you want. This would make a nice gift too.

Tips and Tricks

What are the best photos to use for the marbles? Close-ups work great. Or at least try to find a portion of the photo that you can easily crop so that people can still tell what it is. Remember to have fun thinking what else you could take pictures of next. It would be great to make nature marbles that you could change out each season.

17: Play in the Mud

ADVENTURE SCALE: 2

The basics: Most people avoid mud, but every once in a while it's nice to get a little bit dirty. After a good rain, put on your galoshes and head outside to play in the mud. After you're done, hose yourself off outside for a quick cleaning.

Challenge: Have a mud fight. Yes, it is like a snowball fight but with mud. Keep the game casual and fun. Then after you've thrown the mud all about, you can have a water fight to clean up.

Did you know: Mud can actually be used to create art. You know how mud really sticks on clothes and doesn't want to come out? This is a good thing for art. Consider creating a piece of art out of mud.

18: Go Butterfly Watching

ADVENTURE SCALE: 3

The basics: On a nice summer day, butterflies are busy flying from flower to flower looking for nectar. Use a soft butterfly net to carefully capture one for a few minutes, but then be sure to be gentle. Butterflies are fragile, and you want them to be in good shape when you let them fly away.

Challenge: Try to spot five different butterflies in half an hour. If the butterflies are out and about, it shouldn't be too hard. You can even use binoculars to get great views as butterflies settle onto flowers.

Discover more: Every summer, you can help researchers by counting butterflies in your area. Learn more at butterflycount.org. If you help with this, it'll help conservation efforts around the country.

19: Make Sun Tea

ADVENTURE SCALE: 2

The basics: You can find special sun tea containers at the store, or you can just use a glass jar. Put water in a jar, add five or six tea bags, and then set it out to soak up the sun. If you put it out in the morning, you should have tea ready to drink by the afternoon.

Challenge: While you're making sun tea, pour some lemonade into a plastic ice cube tray and place in the freezer. When the tea is ready, you can mix in lemonade ice cubes for a yummy drink.

Did you know: You can add flavors to your sun tea while it soaks up the sun. Consider throwing in a few slices of lemon or sprigs of herbs. It'll add to the flavor.

20: Have a Nature Stand

ADVENTURE SCALE: 4

The basics: Anyone can have a lemonade stand, but don't stop there. Put together a nature stand with cool rocks, flower photos, and other items you find. Then set up your stand on a sunny day. You can sell lemonade with it, and introduce your neighborhood to your favorite things in nature.

Challenge: Go beyond the basics for your nature stand. For instance, you can make your own mixture for blowing bubbles (see page 97) or you can make trail mix to sell.

Did you know: You could get even more attention for your nature stand at a neighborhood festival. See if there's a fee involved to set up. Then make sure your prices are clearly displayed when you sell your bubbles, flower photos, trail mix, and more. You could earn some summer money.

PICKLES

You don't have to have a lot of expensive canning equipment to make your own pickles. In fact, this is an easy way to pickle any of your summer veggies. So go ahead and pop them in a jar and refrigerate for a few days.

Refrigerator Pickles Serving size: 20

1 cup white vinegar   *1 teaspoon ground turmeric*
1 1/2 cups sugar   *1 teaspoon pepper*
1 teaspoon salt   *1 teaspoon minced garlic*
1 teaspoon mustard seeds   *6 cups cucumbers, thinly sliced*
1 teaspoon celery seeds   *1 cup sliced onions*

Bring all ingredients except the cucumbers and onions to boil over a low heat. Stir gently until the sugar is completely dissolved, which should take about 10 to 15 minutes. Let cool. Meanwhile, mix sliced onions and cucumbers together and place loosely in 1 to 2 jars. Pour liquid mixture over the onions and cucumbers. Seal jar and refrigerate for at least 4 days. Then open them up and give them a try.

More Things to Pickle

Don't like pickles? You can still use the pickling technique to make some other yummy treats. Here are a few vegetables to try pickling. You can either mix them in with the pickles or keep them separate in their own jar.

Asparagus   Beets   Green beans
Onions   Peppers   Carrots

Tips and Tricks

You can also look for pickling recipes that involves "pressure cooking" the jars to seal the lids. This will take a little more practice and help from someone with experience in canning, but it's worth it and gives you another type of pickle to try.

21: Go Mothing

ADVENTURE SCALE: 4

The basics: The first thing to know about searching for moths is that you'll get the best results if you go at night. Put out fruit or a sugary "moth bait" at a simple tray feeder or smear it on a tree in the late afternoon or early in the night. After that you wait for a while. Once it's good and dark, get a flashlight and head out to check your feeders.

Challenge: Get a moth book and try to identify some of those moths. Pick up a book at the local library. Either look for a book that's just about moths or see if there's moth information in a butterfly book.

Bonus video: Want to get tips on how to go mothing at night? Watch a video on this exact subject at destinationnature.net. You can attract some pretty fascinating creatures.

22: Find Snakes Sunning

ADVENTURE SCALE: 3

The basics: Even if you don't like snakes, it's still cool to find them sunning. Snakes often soak up the rays in open areas along trails, on the road, or even on a rock along a river. Observe the snakes from a distance—they like to be left alone.

Challenge: Find a snake's skin. See if you can find a dried up old skin sometime while you're exploring outside. You might either find a whole skin or just part of one. Look at it and observe it. How fresh is it? How much of it is intact? How big is the snake? These are some of the questions to think about.

Did you know: Snakes shed their skins as they outgrow them. Some snakes shed them every few weeks and others don't shed but once a year. As snakes get older, they shed their skins less.

23: Roll Down a Hill like a Log
ADVENTURE SCALE: 2

The basics: Find a great big grassy hill either around your house or at a local park (sledding hills are great options). Then start at the top, cover your face, and start to roll. Giggling is encouraged.

Challenge: Have a race. Make sure the hill is clear of anything that you might run into (ouch!), but then line up and start rolling. Have someone be the one who says "go" and then whoever passes the finish line first is the winner.

Did you know: Since we're on the subject of logs, did you know log rolling is still a sport practiced today? You can find this activity in lots of lumberjack competitions. It's definitely worth seeing in person if there's one in your area.

24: Find Your State Flower
ADVENTURE SCALE: 3

The basics: If you don't know what your state flower is, go online to find out. Then go outside and start looking. Botanical gardens or state parks are great places to look because they will plant natives and state favorites. Don't forget to take a picture once you find it.

Challenge: Did you know there are state trees too? Find out what yours is and see if you can find it. This might seem like it's a lot trickier, but leaf shapes are easier to distinguish than most people think.

Did you know: Not all state flowers are native flowers. Native flowers are those that are native to that specific area, and they're great for planting in your backyard. Learn what plants are native to your area, and make those some of your top choices when planning your garden.

25: Go Fishing

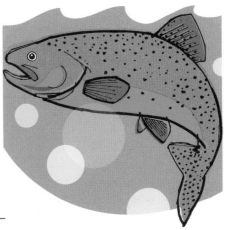

ADVENTURE SCALE: 3

The basics: Get your fishing license, gather up your equipment, and then hit your local lake, pond, or stream. If you don't have your own gear, rent it from a local place. Many states offer free youth fishing days on occasion or host workshops to teach beginners how to fish.

Challenge: Put the timer on and get ready— you must catch ten fish in half an hour. So that's a fish every three minutes. Bait, hook, release. Don't waste time. If that's too much of a challenge, start off smaller (maybe five in half an hour) and then keep increasing your goal.

Bonus video: Want to know the correct way to hold a fish so that it doesn't flop around and poke you with its little spikes? You can master this technique. Learn more at destinationnature.net.

26: Start a Compost Pile

ADVENTURE SCALE: 3

The basics: Take a look at what you throw away every day—chances are you could put much of it into the compost pile instead. If you want to get fancy, buy a full-fledged composting system (the tumbler style is great). Otherwise, start a pile in a simple bin or in the corner of your garden. Mix things like coffee grounds, veggie scraps, and paper with leaves and grass clippings.

Challenge: Try vermicomposting. It's a fancy word for composting with worms. It's pretty cool, though. Worms eat your garbage and poop it into gorgeous soil. Seriously! It might sound a little gross, but it's fantastic soil.

Did you know: The biggest reason compost piles fail is because people put in too many kitchen scraps and not enough brown material. Be sure to give your compost pile a good base of leaves, cardboard, and soil.

PUBLIC GARDENS

Gardeners are some of the friendliest people around. They just want to share the beauty of their work with others. You can find hundreds of public gardens around the country, and often nonprofit groups or volunteers run them. Seek out a couple public gardens in your area or when you're traveling. It's impossible not to appreciate the gorgeous scenes.

Who? Most public gardens are set up for strollers and wheelchairs, so it's really an activity for anyone. Go for an hour or go for the whole day. If the garden you're going to isn't free, check to see if it has a membership you can be a part of. Usually, after only one or two visits it pays off.

What? Public gardens are made for viewing. So expect a lot of walking and watching. If this isn't enough to keep you happy, look at the calendars of public gardens. They often have events, family days, and other special activities. Make plans to go during one of those days for even more excitement.

When? Check the bloom times in your area. Public gardens often have different waves of peak blooming seasons. You might see apple blossoms peak in late spring while the perennials are in their prime mid-summer. Ask the staff or volunteers at the garden. That's what they're there for, and they really do know best.

Where? Botanical gardens are everywhere—so do a search and see if you can find a botanical garden near you. Arboretums or indoor gardens are also something to look for. Of course, you should also explore places like libraries, zoos, and other public places as garden plots are often maintained at these locations too.

Why? Public gardens are a good way to learn about plants and flowers, and you can also see what grows well in your area. Many public gardens plant natives, so go to public gardens for ideas on what to grow in your own backyard. Public gardens often have programs available for locals as well—some are free while others have a small fee. These programs are a good way to learn gardening in your area. Sign up for a couple that interest you.

Tips and Tricks
Don't overlook cafes, restaurants, and other similar locations that might have great gardens. It might not be a public garden in a traditional sense, but it's still worth checking out. You never know where you'll find a great space. If you see a nice garden, ask if you can check it out. They'll probably be thrilled to show you around.

27: Find Your Own Fossils

ADVENTURE SCALE: 3

The basics: Did you know you can find your own fossils just like the paleontologists? Many paleontologists are eager to have visitors on fossil digs. Maybe you can even help dig a little.

Challenge: Go out fossil hunting on your own. You might have to do a little research ahead of time to know what you're looking for and where to look, but it's satisfying to know you did it all by yourself.

Discover more: Head out to a local museum to get an up-close look at fossils. Public museums usually have great fossil collections, and they can help you get started in finding your own.

28: Find an Anthill

ADVENTURE SCALE: 2

The basics: Ants are some of the hardest working insects around. They're always on the move, building and gathering food. Established anthills can be years old and huge. Keep an eye out to see if you can find one in your area.

Challenge: Follow an ant back to its home or see where it's going as it leaves the anthill. It'll take a little patience.

Did you know: Around the world, there are thousands of different kinds of ants. They work hard and carry things on their backs that weigh more than twenty times the amount that they do.

29: Take a Picture from the Top of a Mountain

ADVENTURE SCALE: 5

The basics: Hiking to the top of a mountain is an accomplishment in and of itself, but it's always nice to have an end goal. Once you reach the top, capture that moment with your camera. And, if you can, get a picture with you in it. You'll remember it forever. Make sure your batteries are all charged.

Challenge: Don't just take one picture at the top. Make a photo journal of your entire journey, taking pictures on the way up and the way down. Be sure to get a before and after picture.

Did you know: You can use your camera to take multiple side-by-side pictures from the top of the mountain. Then your computer can edit them together into the full panoramic view from the top.

30: Eat Veggies Straight from the Garden

ADVENTURE SCALE: 2

The basics: Go to your garden, pick a pea, tomato, or whatever else you have growing, and just bite into it right there. Yum! You can't get much fresher than that. Don't worry about dirt. Just brush it off and enjoy.

Challenge: Have lunch or dinner right there in the garden. You might need to pack a sandwich or something to go with the veggies, but take it straight out to the garden, have a seat, and start eating.

Bonus video: If you don't have a big space for sprawling vegetables like cucumbers, then you'll want to see our video. Learn our secret for growing a lot of veggies in a small space at destinationnature.net.

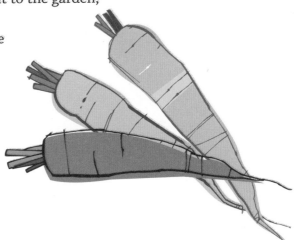

SALSA

Chips and salsa are a summer favorite, especially when you can use fresh garden ingredients. Here are three different salsa recipes to try this summer. But don't be limited by these. Invent your own salsa or add to these recipes. This is the beauty of salsa—everyone likes something different. So use these recipes as guides, but feel free to customize them too. Then grab a couple of bags of chips, invite some friends over, and have a salsa-tasting party.

Watermelon Salsa Serving size: 6
> 2 cups chopped seedless watermelon
> 1/4 cup chopped onion
> 1/4 cup fresh chopped cilantro
> 1/2 teaspoon chili powder
> 1 tablespoon vinegar

Mix all ingredients together. Chill and serve. You can also make a different kind of fruit salsa with this recipe. Just substitute mango or pineapple for the watermelon.

Tomato Salsa Serving size: 6
> 2 cups chopped tomatoes
> 1 large chopped bell pepper
> 2 chopped jalapenos
> 1 small chopped onion
> 1/4 cup fresh chopped cilantro
> 1 teaspoon minced garlic
> 2 limes, juiced

Mix all ingredients together. Chill. The salsa gets better the longer it sits and soaks up the juices of the other ingredients. After an hour or so, taste your salsa and see if you need to add anything to it.

Corn Salsa Serving size: 6

1 1/2 cups fresh roasted corn kernels
1 cup chopped tomatoes
1/4 cup chopped onion
1/4 cup fresh chopped cilantro
1 lime, juiced
1 chopped bell pepper
2 chopped jalapenos
Salt and pepper (optional)

Mix all ingredients together. Add salt and pepper to taste, starting off small first.

Tips and Tricks
With all salsa, let your taste buds be your guide. If you like it hotter, add jalapenos. If you don't like your salsa hot at all, then add sweet peppers and don't use any jalapenos.

31: Go on a Hike

ADVENTURE SCALE: 3

The basics: Sometimes it doesn't matter where you go—just getting outside on a hike and enjoying the world around you is a great way to see your area. Look for hiking trails near you. You'll probably discover something that you never even knew existed.

Challenge: It's easy to hike for an hour or two, but make a whole day of it. Pack your lunch, make sure you have good hiking boots on and any other supplies you might need (like water), and then get going.

Did you know: Some of the most famous hiking trails in North America include the Continental Divide, the Appalachian Trail, and the Pacific Crest Trail. Hikers will sometimes hike these for months at a time, going thousands of miles.

32: Have a Water Fight

ADVENTURE SCALE: 2

The basics: A good water fight always starts with water balloons. It'll take a while to fill them all up, but it's worth it in the end. Make sure you evenly distribute them all to friends. Then ready, set, go! Let the fun begin—keep it friendly.

Challenge: Instead of aiming water balloons at each other, aim for a target. Create a large target out of cardboard. Then take turns seeing who can get the most points with each throw.

Did you know: Most people think they have to fill their water balloons up all the way to be effective. Not true! They'll often burst before you even throw them. Keep them a medium size, and they'll be perfect for throwing.

33: Try Fly Fishing

ADVENTURE SCALE: 4

The basics: You might think fly fishing is just like regular fishing, but it's not. Fly fishing uses artificial "flies" to catch the fish. It'll take a little bit to get the hang of it. Be patient, and get lessons from someone who knows what he's doing. It will definitely take practice.

Challenge: Catch a fish. Sure, you've finally mastered the technique, but now it's time to put those skills to good use. Set a goal of catching at least a one-pound fish.

Did you know: Fly-fishing flies are made of hair and feathers and mimic stoneflies, caddisflies, mosquitos, grasshoppers, or other insects. Some flies can even imitate minnows or mice.

34: Learn to Swim

ADVENTURE SCALE: 4

The basics: Perhaps you learned the basics of swimming when you were a baby, but did you learn any actual form or strokes? For starters, master floating on your back, putting your face in the water. Then try the freestyle stroke and the breaststroke.

Challenge: Now it's time to master the backstroke and the butterfly stroke. Yep, they're a bit more challenging to learn, but give them a try. Either way, they're good practice and get you more and more used to the water.

Did you know: Swimming is one of the best workouts for your body because it's good exercise from head to toe. You can burn up to 500 calories in just an hour.

MARCO POLO

Marco Polo is a fun water game, and you don't need any equipment to play. You just need a group of people that like the water and can swim. This is basically a game of water tag, yet the person who is "it" has to keep her eyes closed, so it makes it even more challenging.

Ages: 5 and up
Materials: None
Length: 20 minutes
Number of players: 5 or more

1. To start, you have to set the rules and make sure that everyone understands them. So first things first—set the boundaries for the swimming area. It works well to make it where everyone can still touch the bottom. Keep in mind that it's better to be too shallow than too deep.
2. Think about what other rules you might want to set. For example, maybe you want to create rules about whether or not people can go underwater, and if so, for how long. You might also want to set a time limit as to how long one person can be "it." It's no fun having the same person chasing everyone else for the whole game, so if after 10 minutes, she hasn't tagged anyone, it's time to rotate.
3. So now that you have the rules set, it's time to start. Choose someone to be it. This person must close her eyes, and count to twenty. No peeking allowed at all! (You're playing on the honor system here.)
4. Everyone else scatters while the it person counts to twenty. Then the it person starts calling out "Marco." After she calls out, everyone else must answer back "Polo." The it person walks and swims around, trying to tag someone. Yet, she keeps her eyes closed the whole time.

5. This game is actually a lot more challenging than it might sound. If you have boundaries set and several people playing, there are only so many places they can go to hide. And it's hard to move fast in water, so eventually, the it person usually tags someone.
6. The person eventually tagged becomes the new "it," and the game continues.

Tips and Tricks

If you happen to be in an area where everyone can't touch the bottom or you're playing with younger kids, it's a good idea to have weaker swimmers wear life jackets. You want everyone to feel safe and secure with this game.

35: Search for an Arrowhead

ADVENTURE SCALE: 3

The basics: Native Americans created arrowheads hundreds or even thousands of years ago. You can find them all across the country, as long as you know where to look. An easy place to look is along rivers and streams. But do a little investigating in your area to learn where other people are finding arrowheads. Then go to those places to look.

Challenge: Look for other Native American artifacts. Pretend you're an archaeologist, and see what you can discover. Go to a state or local Native American museum to see all the things that have been found over the years.

Discover more: Look at your local museum for arrowheads or other artifacts found in your area. You can learn a lot about your state and the people that settled there just by checking out a museum.

36: Try Car Camping

ADVENTURE SCALE: 3

The basics: You don't always need a tent to go camping. Instead, just sleep in your car. Find a campsite to go to, unpack everything you need, and then make a bed in the back of your car. (It helps if your seats fold down.) It's a quick and easy way to enjoy camping. And you'll stay dry even if it rains.

Challenge: Try backpack camping. You'll need a good, solid backpack that can carry everything you need from a tent to campfire supplies. Load everything up, head into the great outdoors, and camp out of your backpack. (Make the oldest or strongest person carry the heavier supplies.)

Discover more: Every year, the National Wildlife Federation leads the Great American Backyard Campout. This usually takes place in June, and they encourage the whole family to camp together. Learn more about this cool event at nwf.org.

37: Watch a Geyser Erupt

ADVENTURE SCALE: 3

The basics: Geysers are pretty rare, and many are located in Yellowstone National Park. A geyser is like a spring, and every so often it erupts, much like a volcano erupts. It's amazing to watch because then you can see how a volcano works.

Challenge: See a famous geyser. The bigger ones tend to be the most famous. Try Old Faithful in Yellowstone. It has impressive eruptions. Don't forget your camera.

Did you know: Geysers need three things to form: heat, water, and rock. Then to erupt, they need the perfect mix of these three things.

STATE AND NATIONAL PARKS

The state and national park systems are some of the best resources in the country for nature lovers. There are thousands of parks scattered all over the country, so stake out the closest ones to you, and then make a goal to visit at least three this year.

They're also good places to visit while on a vacation, even if you're vacationing for the weekend only a few hours away. They're set up for visitors, so take advantage of these great sites in your own backyard.

Who? Parks are especially appealing to older kids. Get a good daypack with lunch, a camera, and whatever else you enjoy. You can even take turns choosing what you want to do. No matter who goes, make sure everyone dresses comfortably and wears good walking shoes.

What? Go hiking, biking, running, walking, birding, animal watching, fishing, exploring, and more. The parks are filled with things just waiting to be discovered. They usually have lots of brochures and ideas with things to do as well. Go out and discover what's available.

When? Most parks are open year-round, though you'll find extended hours in summer. While many areas are easy to get to, don't be afraid to go off the beaten path to explore the lesser-used trails. As long as there's not a sign that it's closed off to the public, feel free to look around.

Where? Your state is your best resource. Look for your local or state tourism website. Chances are, they've highlighted the parks across the state and even have information about what resources are available at each one. If you're visiting some place new or are on vacation, be sure to keep state and national parks in mind. You're bound to discover something new.

Why? State and national parks are owned by the people. Yep, that includes you as well. Here's why—it's usually tax money that keeps these places up and running, so you should visit. You really are part owner of these places, and it's good to see what you're contributing to.

Tips and Tricks
Parks are especially great places to visit at dawn and sunset. The crowds tend to be low, and there's often great activity with birds and wildlife. So get up a little bit early to make it worth your while or wait to go later after everyone else has gone home for the day.

38: Go Mountain Biking

ADVENTURE SCALE: 5

The basics: Mountain biking might sound easy because riding a bike isn't all that difficult. But when you get out there on a bike and you're speeding across the rough terrain, it's hard. If you don't have experience, consider taking a mountain biking tour. They can give you good advice, and they'll have the right equipment to make it a little easier.

Challenge: Bike more than ten miles. This is quite an accomplishment, especially through rough terrain. If ten is too challenging right up front, start with four or five and then build up to ten or more.

Did you know: Road biking and mountain biking are completely different sports that use completely different bikes. Mountain bike trails need the tires to be thick and all-terrain. Road bikes usually have much thinner, smoother tires.

39: Navigate with a Map

ADVENTURE SCALE: 4

The basics: Grab a map of your area, and see if you can find your way to your destination. Pick out a park or natural area you'd like to explore. No cheating and using an online map or using a GPS on a phone or other device.

Challenge: Draw your own map of your neighborhood. What things will you include? Perhaps the bike path and all the bike racks you use. Maybe there is a bird nest you know about. That can go on your map. Be sure to include the compass directions, a scale, and a legend or key.

Did you know: Mapmakers are called cartographers. It can be fascinating to look at historic maps. How has your area changed over the years? Check with your local library or historical society to see if they have old maps on file.

40: Write on Rocks

ADVENTURE SCALE: 1

The basics: Anyone can do this—find a large, sturdy rock. Then find a smaller rock with a pointed tip. Push down hard, and you can write a message. You can try this on a large boulder or just a bigger rock in your neighborhood. The message will likely fade over time, but it's still fun to do.

Challenge: Create some rock art. You can even have a little contest or art show with your friends. See who can put together the best design.

Did you know: One of the most common collections kids start is a rock collection. This is probably because they're so easy to find and save. Start a rock collection saving one rock from each special place you visit.

41: Catch a Crab

ADVENTURE SCALE: 4

The basics: Catching fish is called fishing and catching crab is called crabbing. You can use a piece of string with bait to go crabbing or try a crab cage instead. Either way, it's best to go with someone who has a little bit of experience.

Challenge: Now that you've caught the crab, it's time to eat it. Yes, there is a technique involved, and it might be best to solicit the help of an experienced cook so you can turn it into a tasty meal.

Did you know: Crab festivals are very popular in and around oceanside communities where crabbing is popular and crabs are plentiful. These are great family events, so look for a festival near you.

ROCK ART

It's time to take that rock collection and do something fun with it! Here are two easy projects to make the rocks stars. Good luck, and hopefully these inspire you to create even more unique projects with rocks. Or maybe it'll inspire you to go outside and look for those perfect project rocks.

Rock Side Table

Supplies: Side table, rocks, grout, clear glue
Ages: 7 and up
Time: 45 minutes, plus overnight drying time

How-To:

1. Find a table first. A small end table can be picked up at a second-hand store or rummage sale for as little as $2. Clean it up and paint it your favorite color or leave it as is. If you do paint it, it might take a few layers of paint to really show.
2. Using strong adhesive clear glue, attach your rocks to the top of the table. It helps if the top of the table is even, so you might want to choose rocks that are the same width. This will ensure your top is nice and flat. Make sure all your rocks are stuck on before you move to the next step.
3. Pick up a grout from your local craft store and mix it according to the back of the package. Apply it between the rocks, let dry for the recommended time (usually 15–20 minutes), and then wipe clean with a wet washcloth.
4. Let the table dry overnight. You can fill gaps in, as needed.
5. Now you have a unique table you can use, and best of all, it came from nature.

Rock Name Frame

Supplies: Picture frame, rocks, clear glue
Ages: 5 and up
Time: 20 minutes

How-To:
1. Small rocks work best for this project. Use this excuse to go on a rock hunt and look for tiny rocks that you can arrange in any way you want.
2. Take apart your picture frame and remove the glass. Paint the background (if you want) so the rocks will show up better.
3. Position your rocks before gluing them. You want to make sure you have enough space in the frame.
4. Once you have the rocks where you want them, use a strong adhesive that will dry clear. Apply the glue directly onto the rock and place firmly onto the background of the frame.
5. Let the rocks dry for at least half an hour, and then you'll have a great piece of art. This is a great idea for personalizing for a gift too.

Tips and Tricks
Smooth, even, flat-bottomed rocks will be easiest to work with, especially on the table project. And it's even better if you can find them around the same width so that whatever you set on the table will stay nice and flat. You can often find these kinds of rocks along a stream or a shoreline.

42: Visit a Farmers' Market

ADVENTURE SCALE: 2

The basics: Summer is the perfect time to visit a farmers' market. They'll have almost everything you could hope for, from fruits and veggies to homemade goods, jellies, and more. It's a great way to support your local farmers or community while getting something healthy and tasty too.

Challenge: Try making a meal completely from things you buy at the

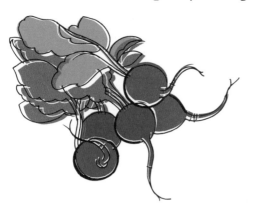

farmers' market. It'll make the shopping more fun, and it's a good challenge. Take a budget (maybe $20) and see if you can do it.

Did you know: Farmers' markets don't just have fruits and veggies. You can also find vendors there with handmade goods. This is a great way to support local artists, farmers, and small business owners. They take a lot of pride in their businesses, and you'll definitely get personalized attention.

43: Try Paddleboarding

ADVENTURE SCALE: 4

The basics: A paddleboard looks like a surfboard, and it comes with a paddle. It's tricky to balance yourself, but with a lot of practice, you'll be able to paddle yourself all over the water.

Challenge: Now try surfing. If you don't have one yourself, rent a surfboard. Then give it a try in the ocean. You can also try body surfing, and you won't need any equipment at all (except maybe a life jacket). You don't even have to go out very far. Just let your body ride in with the waves.

Did you know: You don't have to stand up on a paddleboard or surfboard. As you get used to it, try kneeling on your knees or laying on your belly. This is a good way to practice and get used to being on the water.

44: Run through a Sprinkler

ADVENTURE SCALE: 2

The basics: On a really hot day, you need relief from the heat. Get your bathing suit on, set up a sprinkler, and then zoom through it. Go ahead and invite the neighbors over too. It can be a sprinkler party!

Challenge: Play a game of sprinkler jump rope. It works best if you're using a sprinkler that goes from one side completely to the other side (one that makes a sideways "C" shape). Set up one or two sprinklers, and then see if you can jump so the water doesn't get you. See who can stay the driest.

Did you know: You can make your sprinklers work double duty by positioning them in a spot where you also need to water your garden. You can have fun, and your plants can get a drink.

45: Watch Bats at Sunset

ADVENTURE SCALE: 3

The basics: Just as the sun begins to set for the day, the bats come out, zooming about and looking for mosquitoes and other bugs to eat. They like to zip in and out of open areas, often over water. Put out a blanket to lie down. Then kick back and watch these amazing little creatures.

Challenge: Build or buy a bat house to put up. Yes, they really will use them. Just make sure you hang it high enough in a tree. It might take them a year or two to really find it, so don't give up.

Did you know: Bats have gotten a bad rap over the years. Relatively good eyesight and echolocation (a fancy word for a type of hearing bats use) will help keep them from swooping down into your hair or face. And they're pretty harmless overall.

KICK THE CAN

Ages: 5 and up
Materials: An old can
Length: 10 to 20 minutes per game
Number of players: 4 or more

Kick the Can is one of the oldest and simplest games around. It's like hide-and-seek with a twist. It breaks down into three main parts.

Part 1: To get things started, someone is chosen to be the seeker. Try drawing sticks to decide; the shortest one is the seeker. Keep in mind that it helps when the seeker can run pretty well, so you might not want a younger player to be the seeker or it will be a really short game. Next, the seeker puts a can upside-down in a nice big open area. Then he puts his foot on the can and starts counting to 50 (keep those eyes closed) while everyone runs to hide.

Part 2: After the seeker has counted to 50, he starts to look for all the other players hiding. When he finds someone, the seeker calls the person out by name and then it's a race. If the seeker can get back to the can before the person he found gets there and kicks it, then that person is captured. (The captured players must stay in a designated area near the can. Figure this area out before the start of the game.) If the person beats the seeker, he kicks the can and the seeker has to retrieve it and start counting again.

Part 3: Once the seeker has captured a player, he continues on, searching for more. Meanwhile, the other players try to free the captured. They do this by trying to sneak up and kick the can without the seeker spotting them. This will free any captured players and will force the seeker to start all over again. Also, if someone kicks the can while being chased by the seeker, this too would release the captured. Once all the players are captured, it's time to pick a new seeker and start a new game.

Tips and Tricks

To make it easier, you can play it where the seeker simply has to see a player and call out his name to be captured. It's especially fun and/or challenging to play this game at dusk when it's harder to spot people hiding.

46: Flip Over a Rock

ADVENTURE SCALE: 2

The basics: When you flip over a rock or a log, you never know what you might find underneath. Keep an eye out for any critters that might be mad and defensive that you're disturbing their home, but for the most part, it's a good way to explore nature. Don't forget to put it back where you found it after you're done having a peek.

Challenge: Find a hollow log and take a look inside. Turtles, butterflies, or other bugs and critters could be using it as a home. Just look carefully. You don't want to startle the critters.

Did you know: Piles of rocks, logs, and debris all provide great homes for living creatures. If you're out for a walk or on a hike, remember this, and you'll discover even more. Or create your own pile in the backyard to give animals another habitat source.

47: Pick Summer Berries

ADVENTURE SCALE: 3

The basics: Blueberries, raspberries, blackberries, and strawberries—these are just a few of the berries available for picking during the summer. If you have your own plants, that's great. Otherwise, look for a pick-your-own berries place near you.

Challenge: Make your own jam. It's a fun activity to do as a group, so invite some friends along and make an afternoon out of it. It's easier to do as a group. You have more hands to do the chores, and then you can split it up at the end.

Did you know: Many berries (including strawberries) have two types—Juneberry varieties and everberry. Juneberries are mostly at strawberry farms—they have lots of fruit and produce early. Everberries make good container plants. They produce less fruit overall but will bloom and fruit all summer.

ICE CREAM

Mmmm, nothing says summer like ice cream on a hot day. Making your own ice cream is something everyone should try at least once. With this method, you don't need any machinery at all. You just need energy. Best of all, after you work up a sweat, you can reward yourself with a yummy, cool treat.

Easy Ice Cream Recipe Serving size: 2
1 1/2 cups milk
1 teaspoon vanilla
1/3 cup sugar
1 tablespoon chocolate or strawberry syrup
Ice cubes
Rock salt

Mix the milk, vanilla, sugar, and syrup together in a bowl. Then transfer into either a small can with a secure lid or a quart-size bag. From here, there are two different ways to finish up the ice cream—either by throwing it or rolling it. It does sound a little weird, but that's the beauty of the rock salt. It's really like magic and forms ice cream. Take a look.

Throw It!

Put the quart-size bag with your mixture into a larger, gallon-size bag. In the excess space between the bags, fill with roughly 1/2 cup of rock salt and then fill the rest with ice cubes. Now is the easy part—you just shake it, toss it, and keep it moving as much as possible. It won't be long before the mixture hardens and creates an ice cream–like texture. Depending on how much you're shaking, it could take anywhere from 10 to 20 minutes. Once it's ready, pour in a bowl and eat.

Roll It!

Put your small can into a larger can with a secure lid. Small and large coffee cans work out great. Once the small can is inside the large one, add 1/2 cup rock salt around the edges and fill the rest of the space with ice cubes. Now it's time to roll. Recruit a friend and roll it back and forth. You want to keep it moving as much as possible. After 15 to 30 minutes, you should have a good textured ice cream. Yum.

Tips and Tricks
Once your ice cream is finished, add some of your favorite toppings like summer berries, bananas, jelly, chocolate chips, or sprinkles. Also, try making ice cream with an old-fashioned ice cream machine. It's fun to crank by hand.

48: Try Letterboxing

ADVENTURE SCALE: 4

The basics: Letterboxing is like the ultimate nature treasure hunt. Explorers have been doing this for generations, and it's starting to pick up in popularity again. It combines hiking, navigational skills, and rubber-stamping. There are letterboxes hidden in public areas all over the country.

Challenge: Set a letterboxing goal, and then meet it. For example, this summer, see if you can find twenty new letterboxes in your area. If you're traveling this summer, make it a goal to find letterboxes wherever your travels take you.

Discover more: Like the sound of a nature treasure hunt? If you want to learn more about letterboxing and what it's all about, go to letter boxing.org.

49: Spit Watermelon Seeds

ADVENTURE SCALE: 2

The basics: What do you do with the watermelon seeds in summer? See how far you can spit them. Test out different techniques—using your tongue, take a deep breath and then blow, letting the seed fly off the tip of your tongue.

Challenge: Participate in a seed-spitting contest. You may be able to find a contest at your local fair. Otherwise, just invite all your friends over, mark a line, and get spitting.

Did you know: If you want to do a little practicing, pick up a bag of sunflower seeds. Then find a good ledge and try spitting over it. This will help you practice if you don't have a watermelon immediately on hand.

50: Blow Bubbles

ADVENTURE SCALE: 2

The basics: You can buy bubble solution at the store or make your own by mixing two cups of water with a half cup dish soap and a quarter cup light Karo syrup. You can make your bubbles a color with a little food coloring. Then experiment with making your own bubble wand. A reshaped wire hanger can work great.

Challenge: Create a little game out of your bubbles. See who can blow the biggest one, blow the most, or even pop the most.

Did you know: Blowing bubbles is one of the cheapest activities you can do. Get a big container for a few bucks and then invite a few friends over. If you don't have enough wands for everyone, make your own by shaping wire hangers.

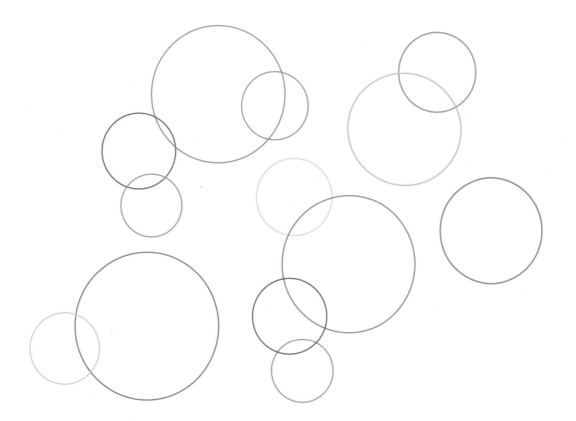

AUTUMN

"I cannot endure to waste anything as precious as autumn sunshine by staying in the house. So I spend almost all the daylight hours in the open air."

—NATHANIEL HAWTHORNE

Autumn is definitely the best season. Think about it—it's the ultimate season for exploration. Everything about fall feels just right. There is a touch of cool in the air, so grab a sweater and head outside. As autumn transitions from warm to cold, what changes do you see in the landscape? Don't hesitate. You'll want to get out there as much as possible before the first snowflakes.

Autumn is harvest season. With a little work and a bit of luck, you'll have fresh produce all season long. You'll also want to can the surplus (or buy from canners at your local farmers' market) to remind you of these flavors all winter. Meanwhile, other produce is still ripening. Apples and pumpkins are autumn favorites.

Small mammals scurry about actively eating, some even storing feed for the winter ahead. Many large mammals are searching for mates in the fall. Autumn rut is in full swing for deer, elk, moose, and bighorn sheep. And keep an eye to the sky. The migration cycle continues as birds begin the journey to their wintering homes.

Fall is the perfect weather to go on a long hike. The scenery has added colors. Nature seems to take on an added urgency in autumn. Fall provides one last chance to see wildflowers in the mountains before snow blankets the landscape.

Cool fall nights make for great sleeping. Pack the tent and the sleeping bags, and go on a final camping adventure. The campfire will seem extra cozy as the sun sets in the autumn.

Autumn adventure awaits. Just open the door, step outside, and let the fun begin.

Autumn's Checklist

☐ 1: Pick a Pumpkin off the Vine

ADVENTURE SCALE: 2

The basics: Anyone can pick out a pumpkin from a pile, but challenge yourself to pick one straight from the vine instead. It might be hard to find someone that will let you pick straight from the vine (many people just place pumpkins in a field for the illusion of picking it yourself), but it's worth the search. Look around and find a place that offers this experience. It'll make decorating it for Halloween even more fun.

Challenge: Grow your own pumpkin and pick it off the vine straight from your backyard. Pumpkins can take a long time to grow (one hundred days or more), so you have to plan ahead.

Did you know: Most county and state fairs have a "largest pumpkin" contest. So if you're feeling ambitious, try growing one for competition. Otherwise, be sure to check out the winners.

2: Find Cocoons or Chrysalises

ADVENTURE SCALE: 3

The basics: Caterpillars are getting ready for winter right now. While some will go underground, you can find those that hide in cocoons and chrysalises in fall. Look under eaves, inside sheds, under limbs and other protected spots. It's not going to be easy to find them, but it's a great treasure hunt.

Challenge: Don't just find those hidden caterpillars; keep track of them. Write down where you found them and then be sure to go back in spring so you can see if you can figure out what they have transformed into.

Did you know: There really is a difference between cocoons and chrysalises. Do you know what it is? Moths make cocoons and butterflies make chrysalises.

3: Find Twenty Different Kinds of Fall Leaves

ADVENTURE SCALE: 3

The basics: Go on a leaf hunt in your backyard or your local park, and look for colorful fall leaves that are all different shapes. Don't take the easy way out. Find leaves that are beautiful, stunning, and unique.

Challenge: Identify all the leaves. You can pick up a tree book at your local library. Look at things like overall size, how many points there are on each leaf, what the color is, and so on.

Did you know: Leaves change their color and drop once the temperatures fall. So if it's a mild autumn, the leaves will take longer to change and fall.

HIKING TRAILS

Hit the trails this season, and take in some great fall color at the same time. Hiking is a year-round activity, but it's especially gorgeous this time of year. It's easy to find hiking trails in your area. There are entire magazines, websites, and stores devoted to this favorite outdoor pastime. Best of all, you can find trails with varying difficulty, so even the youngest outdoor enthusiasts can join.

Who? Anyone can go hiking. Small trails around parks are usually short, well kept, and stroller-friendly if you have younger siblings who need to go along for the ride. It's easy to find more challenging trails for older kids and teens too. Look for difficulty levels (easy, moderate, and difficult).

What? In its most basic form, hiking is just walking. Hiking can be a short leisurely stroll or a multiple-day, backpacking journey. Start off on beginner routes and don't try to do too much. Once you get a little experience, you can do more and more.

When? Hiking can be done year-round (some extreme sports people even love winter hiking). But fall is an ideal time to go because of the cool weather.

Where? If you're new to hiking, try going to your local outdoors store. Ask for good tips on where to go. Also, many states have hiking trails mapped out already. So check your local or state travel site. You'll soon be filled with more hiking trails than you could possibly ever try.

Why? First off, it's a great form of exercise. You can hike for several miles and, because you're always seeing something new and different, you don't even realize it. It's also a great way to go beyond the crowds. Hiking trails are designed to go into areas where there is less overall traffic. So you're likely to see some amazing things in nature that you wouldn't see otherwise.

Tips and Tricks

Many people think hiking is just walking, but it's a lot more work than that. Be prepared—pack snacks that will keep you energized, wear good shoes, and pack plenty of water. And don't forget to take breaks if someone in your group needs a rest. You want to take it easy at first so you have energy to last the entire adventure.

4: Walk a Dog off the Beaten Path

ADVENTURE SCALE: 2

The basics: For many, a dog is a man's best friend. And dogs likely love being out in nature just as much as you do. Reward their loyalty with a nice long walk through a field or the woods. Don't have a dog? Not a problem. Borrow a dog from a friend or get a dog-walking gig. You might even make a little extra money along the way.

Challenge: Walk a cat. (Don't laugh.) Many people are now training their cats to use walking harnesses. Let your cat enjoy the great outdoors, but keep it on a leash to keep your backyard birds alive.

Did you know: Dog parks are growing in popularity every year, and most have plenty of trails to take your furry friend for a walk. This is also a great way to make dog friends with someone, whether you have your own dog or not.

5: Go Owling

ADVENTURE SCALE: 4

The basics: Get your binoculars, bird book, and some flashlights and go out in the woods at night to search for owls. Owls are nocturnal, so the best time to look for them is at night. Gather up some friends and look for an organized owl hunt at a local nature center or bird observatory to make it even more fun.

Challenge: Train yourself to listen first and decipher what owl you're hearing. If you can hear an owl first and figure out where the noise is coming from, this will also help you in your search.

Did you know: Learn how to mimic their calls, and you can bring some owls in close. Use this on a limited basis, though. You don't want to confuse the owls.

☐ 6: Hang Upside Down from a Tree

ADVENTURE SCALE: 3

The basics: Safety first with this one—make sure you have someone to spot you. But find a good tree in your area, climb it (not too high), and then dangle upside down by your legs. You'll see the world from a whole new point of view.

Challenge: Find a tree with a great view so that when you hang upside down you really get a unique perspective. For example, a view of a lake or flower field would be really pretty.

Did you know: Grapevines (or other tree vines) in the forest can make fun swings. Make sure the vines are secure and then sit on them like a swing and gently rock back and forth.

☐ 7: Pick Fall Raspberries

ADVENTURE SCALE: 2

The basics: Raspberries are ripe in early summer and then there's also a second harvest time in early fall. Look for a pick-your-own raspberry place in your area. You can pick (and even taste test a few) to buy for a reasonable price. Remember to watch out for thorns.

Challenge: Take those raspberries and make some jam or a pie with them. Or if you're feeling really adventurous, try making a torte. (Tortes just sound fancy. They aren't that hard.)

Did you know: Plan ahead when planting raspberry plants. Some produce berries in spring, while others don't produce until late summer or fall. You can also find thornless plants that only grow a couple feet high. So do a little research first.

TWIG ART

As you're out hunting for gorgeous leaves that have fallen to the ground, keep an eye out for the perfect sticks to use for some art projects. Generally, you want to find twigs that aren't too thick and are less than a foot long. You don't want them to be too short either. The perfect sticks would be about 8–10 inches long. Gather up a few dozen, and then try one of these projects.

Twig Picture Frames

Supplies: Twigs, picture frame, glue
Ages: 3 and up
Time: 20 minutes

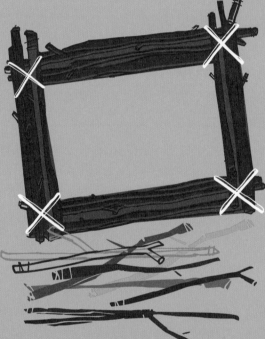

How-To:

1. It's easiest to use a picture frame you already have at home. Chances are you have one that has an old picture or another one in a cabinet somewhere that you've never used.
2. Cover the top of the picture frame with a thin layer of glue. You don't need much. Just gently smear the glue over the frame with your finger.
3. Fill the frame with layers of twigs. You are making a twig mosaic, so you'll have to trim the twigs a little bit to make them all fit perfectly.

Tips and Tricks

Don't have a frame? Here's an alternative—create your own frame out of cardboard. Then you can hang it with string from the back. If you're really feeling creative, don't use a frame or cardboard as a base at all. Find four twigs and brace them together using string or wire to make a square frame.

Supplies: Twigs, art canvas or picture frame, glue
Ages: 6 and up
Time: 15 minutes

1. Decide what you want your art to be displayed on. You can pick up an art canvas from an arts and crafts store. Or take the glass out of a picture frame and use that background (it's usually some sort of thick cardboard).
2. If you choose, paint your canvas or background a solid color. This will help the sticks show up better. You could also paint it in two tones—perhaps a green on the bottom quarter and blue on the top three quarters would help create a grass and sky scene.
3. Using your twigs, create a piece of art. Secure the twigs with glue that will dry completely clear. You can either make your art abstract (meaning you're not really trying to create specific objects) or try creating a scene.
4. Once your piece of art is done, hang it inside or out to enjoy nature. If you do hang it outside, make sure you hang it under an eave so it's protected.

Tips and Tricks
You might want to pencil out your design first before gluing on the twigs. You could also lay out all of the twigs first and then glue on the pieces one at a time.

8: Watch the Leaves Fall

ADVENTURE SCALE: 1

The basics: This is going to take patience more than anything. Make yourself stop, relax, unwind, and just watch the leaves fall. On a nice day, take a chair and/or a picnic lunch to your local park, and then enjoy the simplicity of the day.

Challenge: Turn it into a game by seeing who can guess how many leaves will fall in half an hour. If you want an even closer view, get right under the tree. Maybe some will even fall on you.

Discover more: You can find dozens of leaf games, craft projects, and more online. Search with your parents, and find a few things to try as a whole family.

9: Save Your Own Seeds

ADVENTURE SCALE: 3

The basics: Did you have a favorite vegetable or flower this year? Save the seeds, and you can plant them next spring. If you don't have any seeds yourself, ask any gardeners you might know to see if they have any to spare. For fruit and veggie seeds, just take them out fresh and dry them. For flower seeds, wait for the plants to start drying and then save the seeds.

Challenge: Save at least five different seeds this fall and get them to germinate and grow next spring. You can even make your own little envelopes using paper and some tape.

Bonus video: Saving seeds is really easy. Learn an easy technique for this by going to destinationnature.net.

10: Build Your Own Scarecrow

ADVENTURE SCALE: 4

The basics: This activity is a great reason to hit your local thrift store or rummage sales for scarecrow pants, a shirt, and even shoes or a hat. Stuff the shirt and pants with straw, grass clippings, or whatever else you have. Be creative and see what you can come up with using recycled materials.

Challenge: Hold a scarecrow challenge in your neighborhood to see who can come up with the best design. Have everyone be in charge of one thing. Buying the supplies all at once is easier and will save money.

Did you know: The original scarecrow was designed to scare crows away from farmers' fields. These tactics only work for so long, though. Eventually, the birds get used to them and come back anyway.

11: Plant Garlic

ADVENTURE SCALE: 2

The basics: Garlic is a bulb and thus it does best if you plant it in the fall and let it grow over winter. Get bulbs from your local garden center and plant roughly three inches deep, three to six inches apart, and in full sunlight. Water initially but then as winter sets in, just ignore the plants until they start growing in spring.

Challenge: While there are two main types of garlic, hard-necked and soft-necked, there are dozens of varieties. In addition to the popular types, experiment with some lesser-known varietals like the purple stripe ones.

Did you know: Garlic is used in dozens of dishes, including spaghetti. You crush it up to really pull out the flavor. Like onions, garlic can be stored for several months before you use it.

CAPTURE THE FLAG

Capture the Flag is a game of team pride. You need at least 4 people on each team and at least 3 teams to really make it a good game. It also really helps if you have a good amount of space for people to play. Keep in mind that this game could go really fast or it could take a lot of time. Don't rush through it, though. Strategize and put a plan together.

Ages: 6 and up
Materials: 2 flags, markers to decorate
Length: 1 hour or more
Number of players: 12 or more

1. When you play Capture the Flag, you first have to create a flag. Each team makes their own (teams can be made up of 2 to 6 players each). As you create your team name and flag, take a lot of pride in it. This is what you'll be protecting, so take a little extra time with it.
2. Once all the flags are created, the teams find a spot to place them. It has to be out in the open, but think about placement a little bit first. Where you put your flag could have a big impact on how you do in the game.
3. Now it's time for the game to begin. The point of the game is to capture other team flags while protecting your own. Again, this is where strategy comes into play. Will you send two people to go look for other flags while another couple stay back to guard your flag? If you're protecting your own flag, you must stay at least 20 feet away at all times. You can't sit next to it.
4. If someone steals your flag and then you tag her, she has to give it back.
5. Whichever team still has its flag at the end and has the most flags of other teams is the winner.

Tips and Tricks

You can decide as a group how long you want the game to go on and how many points you get for keeping your flag protected versus capturing others. Once the flags are out, a good rule is to set a timer for 30 minutes or an hour.

12: Collect Acorns

ADVENTURE SCALE: 2

The basics: Acorns are the seeds of oak trees, and many different species of oak trees are found throughout much of the United States. Acorns are also a popular food source for many different species of wildlife including squirrel, deer, wild turkey, and wood ducks. Try gathering some acorns and offering them in the wild to see what animals you can attract.

Challenge: Make acorn people using toothpicks and different sizes of acorns. It might take a little work to get the toothpicks to stick inside the acorns, but try a few different spots until you get it to work.

Did you know: You really can grow a whole tree from a single little acorn. It's going to take some time, but try potting an acorn to see if you can get a baby tree started.

13: Make Pinecone Feeders

ADVENTURE SCALE: 2

The basics: You've probably seen them before—those pinecone feeders that everyone makes for the birds. Yep, they really are easy. Just fill with peanut butter and then roll in birdseed.

Challenge: Find a unique way to display these feeders, possibly strung in a row or hung from a wreath. You could also display them vertically with string. No matter how you hang them, the birds are sure to be happy.

Did you know: Pinecones aren't the only things from nature you can use to make your own feeder. Try tying several small twigs together and smearing peanut butter across them. And look around to see what else you can find. Be creative!

☐ 14: Read a Book under a Tree

ADVENTURE SCALE: 1

The basics: This task is simple—all it requires is the right tree, the right book. and a gorgeous fall day. Look for a straight and sturdy tree that is at least wider than your shoulders and has a good canopy to keep you shaded while leisurely turning the pages.

Challenge: Find more places in or around the backyard to chill out, relax, and read. A little nook in the garden, a hammock, on a large rock near a stream—all of these are great options.

Discover more: Most libraries offer reading programs that you can participate in to earn prizes. See if your community supports something like this or look online for national reading rewards programs as well.

☐ 15: Collect Your Own Campfire Wood

ADVENTURE SCALE: 2

The basics: Nothing is better on a cool fall night than the warm glow of a campfire. While firewood stands are convenient and sometimes necessary options, for many camping locations, collecting your own is a fun alternative.

Challenge: Light a fire with one match. The trick is to have patience and lots of kindling, small twigs, and branches. The teepee method of stacking the kindling is the best. You want to give the fire some air, but you also want to keep it protected at the same time.

Did you know: Never transplant firewood from one place to another. Harmful insects and plant diseases can be spread this way. So if you collect your own, make sure you do it from the nearby woods.

16: Listen to the Howl of a Wolf

ADVENTURE SCALE: 3

The basics: Perhaps nothing is as iconic as a wolf howling in the wild. The upper Midwest, including areas of northern Wisconsin and Minnesota, offers up the chance to experience a wolf howl, as do small pockets of the Southwest and Southeast, and a few national parks in the West.

Challenge: Do a little wolf research—Yellowstone National Park has many packs, and it's one of the best places to see (and hear) this great animal. These are some pretty amazing animals.

Discover more: Some of the most studied wolves in the world can be found on Isle Royale in Lake Superior. Learn more about this important study at isleroyalewolf.org.

17: Create a Fall Flower Display

ADVENTURE SCALE: 2

The basics: Fall is a great time for plants. Mums take center stage, but don't overlook ornamental peppers, swiss chard, kale, ornamental grasses, and pansies. It's a great excuse to go to the local garden center to see what options they have.

Challenge: Create a couple of gorgeous fall containers with plants like mums and pansies that can take a little bit of frost. If you plant them early in fall, they will likely last to Halloween and even longer.

Did you know: This is the time of year to plant spring-blooming bulbs. Get out there and plant your tulips, hyacinths, and daffodils. And it's not too late to add in a few perennials that you pick up cheap at the garden center.

CAMPGROUNDS

Ah, camping. You can hardly find a cheaper family trip. You can get as involved as you want—packing dozens of supplies to make your own meals, building your own campfire, etc. Or you can also take an easier route and just focus on the basics. Camping is a good reminder to unplug every once in a while—take a book or board games and just enjoy the time in the great outdoors with your family.

Who? People camp with kids at any age—even babies. However, kids age 5 and up are probably going to do best out in a tent. They can stay up later, roasting marshmallows on the fire, and they won't mind sleeping on the ground in a sleeping bag. Make it an activity for the entire family. Or if you're not seasoned campers, try camping in your backyard before you hit up a campground.

What? You can find very simple campgrounds with almost no amenities or you can find elaborate sites with activities, water play areas, grill areas, and more. Find out what amenities you'd like to have, and then do a little bit of research before you go. The areas with more activities are naturally going to be a bit more crowded, but it's worth it if you're looking for things like beach areas and showers. If you like being secluded, find an area that's more remote.

When? Many campgrounds are open year-round, but late spring to early fall is going to be when they are most popular. You really can't pick a wrong time to go, but keep in mind that you don't want it to be too hot or cold. And plan accordingly depending on what time of year you're going—don't forget things like bug spray and extra blankets.

Where? It's never been easier to find campgrounds near you. Not only does every visitor center and travel website have a specific section for campers, but there are also dozens of resources online to choose from. Just type in "camping" along with your destination (by city or state) and then see what comes up. Chances are you'll have results in an instant.

Why? Nothing makes you appreciate nature like being out in it 24 hours a day. When you go camping, nature is all around you. Even if you don't think you're the camping type, give it a try for at least a night. You might like it more than you think.

Tips and Tricks
Start off small—if you haven't been camping with your family, just do an overnight trip. If they love it, keep increasing the length of time you go. You might soon be going for weeklong trips all over the country. But it's important not to overdo it right away. One night sleeping in a wet tent because of rain could make someone never want to try camping again, and you don't want that.

Bonus Video
Get tips for creating a long-lasting campfire at destinationnature.net.

18: Listen to Your Echo Bounce off Canyon Walls

ADVENTURE SCALE: 2

The basics: Walk to the edge of a canyon. Peer over the edge, and let loose. Give out the biggest yell you can muster, and listen to your echo bouncing off the canyon walls.

Challenge: Anyone can yell out an echo, but do you have what it takes to yodel off the canyon walls? Practice your yodeling, and then when you're ready, go find out.

Did you know: Most canyons have been carved out because of rivers. Look at how the canyon curves and see how it matches the curve of the river below. It's almost like a great big piece of art.

19: Bob for Apples

ADVENTURE SCALE: 2

The basics: Bobbing for apples is as American as, well, apple pie. Apple festivals and community carnivals offer up the activity, but it is simple enough to host your own apple bobbing with your friends. Just fill up a bucket with water, apples, and then bob away.

Challenge: Place a mix of green and red apples and then target a specific apple. This is really difficult. Then have someone time you as to how long it takes. Offer prizes for the best bobbers.

Did you know: This tradition doesn't just take place in America. In Scotland, the game is called Dooking, and in Ireland, the game is called Snap Apple.

❑ 20: Conquer a Corn Maze

ADVENTURE SCALE: 3

The basics: Test your hamster instincts as you try to find your way
through the corn stalks that tower above you. Maize mazes are a popular fall activity throughout much of the country. Some farmers even
cut elaborate shapes into their fields using GPS technology and fancy
tractors.

Challenge: Some corn mazes become haunted during the weeks leading up to Halloween. Finding your way out of the corn is impressive
enough, but true adventurers will do it while being attacked by scare-
crows from behind the corn stalks.

Did you know: Corn is easy to grow. Choose to grow the traditional yellow variety or also look for purple, red, or multicolored versions. If it's
too late to grow corn this year, pick up some seeds on clearance to try
next year.

❑ 21: Harvest Pecans

ADVENTURE SCALE: 3

The basics: Pecans are ready for harvesting in fall. It's a simple process
but can take a little time. First, you put down tarps, and then you use
a long stick to knock the pecans loose from the branches (some people
call this frailing). Then you pick through the pecans, sorting out the
good from the bad.

Challenge: Crack your pecans and then roast them or dice them up and
use them in a recipe. Try making up your own recipe with certain spices
or herbs. Or you could just eat them straight. Fresh nuts are the best.

Did you know: Frailing is a really weird word that is hard to trace
back to its origin. Ken swears Stacy made it up, but she insists she
grew up frailing pecan trees in Oklahoma. (Her mom backs her up on
this as well.)

TRAIL MIXES

Hit the hiking trails this fall with your own trail mix creation. The best thing about making your own trail mixes is that you can mix and match as much as you want. Don't like peanuts? Leave 'em out! Love dried fruit? Load it up!

Here's a basic recipe, but mix and match as much as you want.

Serving size: 15 half-cup servings

> *1 cup of something fruity*
> *1 cup of something sweet*
> *1 cup of something nutty*
> *1/2 cup of something fun*
> *4 cups of something crunchy*

Mix all the ingredients together. You can choose more than one fruity, sweet, or nutty item if you'd like to make up the full cup. The same with the crunchy and fun items—mix them up or use just one.

Something Fruity
Raisins
Dried apple pieces
Dried cranberries
Dried cherries
Dried bananas

Something Sweet
M&Ms
Chocolate chips
Chocolate-covered raisins
Chocolate-covered peanuts

Something Nutty
Peanuts
Pecans
Walnuts
Almonds

Something Crunchy
Cheerios
Chex
Pretzels
Crackers

Something Fun
Miniature marshmallows
Sunflower seeds
Wasabi peas
Dried mango, chopped

Tips and Tricks
When it comes to trail mix, there's really no right or wrong. You might be tempted to put in lots of sweet items, but remember a little goes a long way. This will keep it healthier too.

22: Volunteer for a Local Nature Group

ADVENTURE SCALE: 3

The basics: Nature is everywhere, and so are nature organizations. From a small downtown urban metropark to an expansive wilderness area, volunteers are useful to most every nature group. While some of the tasks will be indoor duties, dedicated volunteers often get to experience some amazing outdoor activities. Perhaps a local bird bander could use assistance. Maybe you'd enjoy leading a nature walk to share your love of nature, and inspire others. Or you could take part in the annual cleanup efforts in your area.

Challenge: Take part in a fundraising effort for a nature organization. It might be more work, but then you can see the money go right back into the community. It's one of the best ways to give back on a local level.

Did you know: Most of these nature groups run on very small staff and budgets. They couldn't survive without volunteers, so take a minute to see what you can do. They'll probably help you as much as you help them.

23: Watch the Sun Set

ADVENTURE SCALE: 1

The basics: Every morning it rises in the east, and every evening it sets in the west. Get out there and watch it. It sounds simple, but it's worth taking the time to do it. Be sure to take your camera to snap a picture.

Challenge: The earth tilt is what gives us the seasons. It is fun to watch the sunset shift along the horizon as the seasons come and go. Watch the sunset from the same location throughout the year, and you'll be able to detect this shift.

Did you know: For sunrise, sunset, moonrise, and moonset times, check out timeanddate.com. This easy-to-use site offers quick, useful information.

24: Go on a Full Moon Hike

ADVENTURE SCALE: 4

The basics: The harvest moon is the full moon closest to the autumn equinox. The bright light of the full moon makes it a great time for a walk. Pack a flashlight, bug spray, and go exploring. Of course, it's best to go with a small group—not on your own.

Challenge: Camp out under a full moon. You'll be amazed at how light it really is outside. You might not even need a flashlight at all, especially if it's a clear night. Be sure you have a nice thick sleeping bag since it can start getting pretty cool at night in fall.

Bonus video: Get some secret tips for making the most out of a hike, whether you're headed out at night or during the day. Learn more at destinationnature.net.

25: Sit in a Tree Stand

ADVENTURE SCALE: 3

The basics: Hunters often use tree stands to sit quietly waiting for their quarry to pass. Tree stands can be very high up, so you can't just go climbing random stands you find. Make sure you're with someone experienced. Although you'll be high above the ground, wild animals have great senses and can still detect your presence unless you remain quiet and still. Your patience will be rewarded by great looks at all types of wildlife, from squirrels and deer to hawks and turkeys.

Challenge: Take your camera along and capture the wildlife with it while you sit. Most people sit in tree stands early in the morning, and this is one of the best times to see and photograph wildlife.

Did you know: Some photographers use tree stands as photo blinds. (Photo blinds are camouflaged areas where you can hide as a way to get close-up pictures of wildlife.) Photographers also use photo blinds that look a lot like tents that just sit on the ground.

26: Soak in a Hot Springs

ADVENTURE SCALE: 2

The basics: Hot springs are geothermal features most abundant out in the West. Some are commercial operations, while others are more natural. Some of the best require hiking to. They all have comfortable warm waters that are especially relaxing as the cool temperatures settle in.

Challenge: Experience hot springs on a cold day. The change from cold to hot is shocking yet relaxing. Once you step into the water, you'll forget all about the frost and chill.

Did you know: Hot springs are a result of geothermal heated groundwater. This sounds complicated, but they're just bodies of water that are heated from the Earth's crust. Still, it's pretty amazing that it doesn't take any machines or electricity to make this natural hot tub.

27: Ride a Horse

ADVENTURE SCALE: 5

The basics: Horseback riding lets you experience nature from a whole new perspective. Trail rides are popular on western trails, while a horseback ride along the beach can also be fun. Look for a place in your area that offers this experience. It's one you won't forget.

Challenge: Ride a donkey. They have a reputation for being stubborn, but they're actually great to ride. Donkeys can be more sure-footed than their larger cousins, and they are the preferred beast of burden along the Grand Canyon.

Did you know: When it comes to riding horses, it's all about confidence. Any good rider will tell you that your horse can sense nervousness. Work on being cool, calm, and confident, and you'll be a natural rider.

FLASHLIGHT TAG

You can do a lot with a flashlight, and it's especially fun when you can turn it into a game. This takes the classic game of tag and mixes in a little bit of hide-and-seek. Make sure everyone has a good working flashlight before you get started. Then let the fun begin!

Ages: 3 and up
Materials: Flashlights
Length: 15 minutes per game
Number of players: 2 or more

1. With every good game of tag, you need a home base. This is where the "it" person counts at the beginning. And it's also a safe haven if some players need a rest. (Of course, you might have to make a rule that you can't stay at home base more than a minute.)
2. To get started, everyone except the person who is it runs to hide, carrying their flashlights with them.
3. Once the person who is it counts to 30, he sets out to hunt the hidden players. Here's where the game is like tag. In order to find someone, you have to "tag" the person with your flashlight beam, right on the chest.
4. If you spot someone, you absolutely have to tag him on his chest to actually make it count. If you flash your beam on his leg but then he runs to home base before you can get him on the chest, then he's safe.
5. Once you find someone, he then helps you find the other hidden players with his flashlight. This game is especially fun with a large group, especially when you have 5 or 6 players, all searching for the last couple of hidden players with their flashlights.

Tips and Tricks

This game is perfect for cool autumn temperatures. Put on a jacket and head outside right at dusk. If you want to make it easier to know when people tag you, use masking tape to make the X on everyone in the same spot. Then when the flashlight hits it, you'll know for sure that you've been hit!

28: Find Migrating Monarchs

ADVENTURE SCALE: 3

The basics: While some butterfly species overwinter in caterpillar form, a few species actually migrate. The monarch migration is a multiple generation affair. While ranging from southern Canada and much of the northern United States during the summer, the monarch's communal wintering grounds are found in the highlands of Mexico and sections of California.

Challenge: Grow your own milkweed, the monarch host plant, to encourage these delicate friends to visit your backyard. This is very important to keep the monarch population alive—they've actually been declining. So do your part and plant milkweed.

Bonus video: Learn how to recognize milkweed in the wild, and get tips for growing this native in your own garden. Learn more at destination nature.net.

29: Plant Cool Season Vegetables

ADVENTURE SCALE: 2

The basics: Gardening isn't just for summer. The backyard harvest can continue well into the fall if you plant some hardy cool season vegetables. Favorites include kale, chard, and salad greens like arugula, mustard, and leaf lettuces. Root vegetables are also a good choice including carrots, turnips, radishes, and beets.

Challenge: Experiment with a cold frame to extend the season even further. You can buy one or look for instructions online to build your own.

Did you know: If you start growing a second crop and then frost starts to set in, you can cover your veggies with ordinary sheets at night. Then remove the sheet in the warmth of the day. If they're in containers, you can just bring them inside but keep them near a sunny window.

30: Witness Shorebird Migration

ADVENTURE SCALE: 4

The basics: While many species of birds migrate, many of the shorebird species are champions of long distance travel. You'll have to be on the ball to see this—most start their migration in later summer. So have your binoculars ready.

Challenge: See if you can ID some of these birds. It can be a bit tricky, but a good field guide can help. Don't just look for specific marks—make sure you look at body size, wing shape when flying, and other similar details.

Did you know: You're not just going to see birds near the shore. Go inland a bit, and you'll find dozens of other migratory birds passing through. They might not be their traditional coloring as some birds molt (change feathers) in fall. But it's still amazing to see some new or unusual fliers.

31: Watch Bugling Elk

ADVENTURE SCALE: 3

The basics: The second largest member of the deer family in North America, male elk have a unique fall tradition called bugling that you can hear if you're in the right place at the right time. The species is abundant in many of the national forests and national parks of the West, but has also been reintroduced into many central and eastern states including Kentucky, Michigan, and Pennsylvania.

Challenge: Learn to make the elk bugle with your own voice or with an elk call. Resist the temptation to bugle at wild elk unless you are a licensed elk hunter.

Did you know: Male elk will use their huge antlers to challenge one another during mating season. Chances are you won't get to witness it in the wild yourself, but you could look up a video of it with your parents online.

NATURE CANDLES

Half the fun of this project is finding the objects to go in it. Seashells are one of the best and easiest things to put down into candles—what a great way to remember that vacation to the beach. You don't need a lot. Just a few items will go a long way. Take a look at how to make these beach-themed nature candles.

Supplies: Jar, candle gel, wick, sand, seashells, candle scent
Ages: 6 and up
Time: 20 minutes

How-To:

1. Get all your supplies. Things you want to think about: Make sure the wick you buy is long enough for your jar. You want to have at least an inch of wick beyond the top of the jar. You also want to make sure to get a clear gel so you can see your objects in the candle.
2. Pour about an inch or two of sand in the bottom of the jar. Place your seashells in the bottom, leaving a place for the wick in the center.
3. Heat up your gel, following the directions on the container. Don't overheat!
4. Whatever candle scent you chose, stir a few drops in with a spoon. Take a little sniff, and if you don't smell it, add a few more drops.
5. Place your wick in the center of the jar and have someone hold it in place.
6. This is where you have to be careful. The person who is holding the wick needs to be still. Then have an adult pour the hot gel gently into the jar, making sure she steers clear of the helper.
7. Don't touch the jar! But you do want to hold up the wick while the gel starts to set. This is a boring job, but you'll want to hold it for about 10 minutes. By this time, the gel will start to solidify.

8. Wrap the top of the wick around a pencil and let it rest across the top of the jar. Let it sit there for a couple of hours, making sure the wick doesn't try to bend too much.

9. After the gel has completely settled, trim the wick so that you only have a small piece left.

10. Light your candle and enjoy your new creation.

Tips and Tricks

Try a few other nature-related objects in the bottom of your candle. For instance, pinecones or rocks look nice. Go on a hike or collect things over the various seasons, and then when it's time to make your candles, go to your nature stash to see what's available. These candles also make a nice gift. If you're buying supplies to do 1 or 2, you might as well buy a few extra supplies to make 5 or 6. Then give them away to family and friends for the holidays.

32: Jump on a Pile of Leaves
ADVENTURE SCALE: 2

The basics: This one is easy for residents of much of the eastern half of the United States. As deciduous trees lose their leaves in the fall, piles of leaves in the yard become irresistible playgrounds for children of all ages. Make a big, huge pile and then take a giant leap.

Challenge: Compost the leaves. The leaves can be combined with other organic matter for your compost bin. You can also put them around your perennials to help protect them over winter.

Did you know: Have you ever looked at the veins of a leaf? Take a close look, perhaps even under a microscope. It's pretty amazing to see the details. Each one is a little bit different, so you could even compare them side by side.

33: Go Apple Picking
ADVENTURE SCALE: 2

The basics: Find an apple tree and harvest the fruits. With dozens of varieties available at most orchards, you're sure to find one that suits your taste buds. Apples can be sweet, tart, and downright sour. What do you prefer? And here's a quick hint for when you go apple picking—take or rent a wagon. If you get a big bag, it's quickly going to be too heavy to carry!

Challenge: Make your own applesauce and apple pie from the apples you picked from the orchard. Look for a good recipe online or ask around the family to see if there are recipes that have been passed down.

Did you know: You can find a lot of dwarf apple trees these days that are perfect for planting in the backyard. If you plant an apple tree now, you could actually have apples next year.

☐ 34: Eat Local for an Entire Day

ADVENTURE SCALE: 2

The basics: Fall is a good time of year for eating local cuisine. Start your day with farm fresh eggs, and then see what else you can eat. Perhaps local for you is a harvest from the sea. Or it could be beef from the country farm. Perhaps you need to pay a visit to your local farmers' market. Vendors offer up all of your culinary needs for local eating.

Challenge: Take local to an extreme level. Eat from your own garden for the day. If you can't make all your meals just from your garden, then do the next best thing—use something from your garden for all your meals. A tomato in a salad or some steamed carrots are good side dishes.

Discover more: Look for restaurants in your town that support local farms. They usually advertise this on their websites or on their doors. It's another way to eat local.

☐ 35: Dry Gourds

ADVENTURE SCALE: 2

The basics: Gourds are related to cucumbers, squash, melons, and pumpkins. They can be quite easy to grow. There are many different kinds available—large, small, fun shapes, bright colors—so look for one that speaks to you. (If it's too late to plant your own, look for gourds to buy at a local farmers' market.)

Challenge: Turn a gourd into a birdhouse. Make sure you don't make a hole that is too big. Wrens and chickadees are especially fond of gourd houses, and the hole should be just over an inch wide.

Did you know: Gourds are versatile. Cut off the top and make a bowl out of it. Put drainage holes in the bottom and use it as a container. Draw a face on it and light the inside for Halloween. What else can you think of?

APPLES

It's apple season, which means it's also the perfect time to fill your house with the fresh aroma of baking. Go out and pick your own apples, and then get to work peeling and slicing in the kitchen. Apple pie is an obvious choice, but here are a few more ideas to go beyond the ordinary.

German Apple Cake Serving size: 10

2 cups flour
1 teaspoon baking soda
1 teaspoon salt
1/2 teaspoon cinnamon
3 eggs, beaten
2 cups sugar
1/2 cup oil
1/2 teaspoon vanilla
5 cups peeled and sliced
   apples
1/2 cup raisins (optional)

Sift together flour, soda, salt, and cinnamon. Set aside. Combine eggs, sugar, oil and vanilla. Beat until well blended. Add dry ingredients and mix well. Fold in apples and raisins. Put into greased pan and bake at 350°F for an hour or until apples are tender.

Apple Crisp Serving size: 10

5 cups peeled and sliced apples
3/4 cup sugar
3 tablespoons cornstarch
1 1/2 cups quick oats
1/2 teaspoon salt
1/3 cup olive oil
1/2 cup maple syrup
1/4 cup flour
1/4 cup chopped walnuts
1 teaspoon vanilla

Fill a 9x9-inch pan with apples. Mix sugar and cornstarch together and sprinkle over apples. Mix the rest of the ingredients together and sprinkle over top of apples. Bake at 350°F for 1 hour or until apples are tender.

Applesauce Serving size: 8

5 cups apples, peeled and sliced
1 teaspoon cinnamon
1/2 cup sugar
1 tablespoon lemon juice

Place apples in a medium pan and barely cover with water. Simmer over medium heat for about 20 minutes. Let apples cool and run them through a blender. Then add cinnamon, sugar, and lemon juice. Cook another 5 minutes over medium heat. Let cool and enjoy.

Tips and Tricks

When you go to an apple orchard, be sure to check with them to see if they have any recipes. They'll often have their best family recipes for apple pie, applesauce, and more. These recipes are definitely worth trying.

36: Make Your Own Nature Costume

ADVENTURE SCALE: 4

The basics: Fall is the time of year for costumes. Halloween, harvest festivals, and Celtic celebrations are all great reasons for putting on a costume. Be creative this year. Construct a costume out of natural items.

Challenge: Dress up as your favorite nature animal. For instance, you can create your own bird, butterfly, or bunny costume. What other ideas can you come up with?

Discover more: You can find oodles of costume ideas online, and most focus on making it for free or for very little. If you have an idea of a nature-related costume you want to try, Google it with your parent.

37: Go Geocaching

ADVENTURE SCALE: 5

The basics: Geocaching is a modern day scavenger hunt. People hide caches and then others use GPS to find the cache. With a quick Internet search, you can find countless geocaches near you. Plug the coordinates into your GPS, and you are ready to go.

Challenge: Create your own geocache. Just make sure you follow regulations when hiding geocaches. They are prohibited on some public lands, and you should always respect private property rights. Local nature centers are often encouraged to have geocaches located on their preserves.

Discover more: To get involved in geocaching, you'll probably find yourself at geocaching.com at some point or another. It's a good way to get started and an impressive site.

38: Whistle on a Blade of Grass

ADVENTURE SCALE: 1

The basics: Pluck a nice long blade of grass. Hold it between your thumbs, skinny side out, pucker up, and make sweet grass music. Now don't give up if you can't get it to whistle right away. You might just need a little practice or perhaps a bigger blade of grass. Keep trying, and your hard work will pay off.

Challenge: Team up with some friends and whistle out a song on your grass instruments. Yep, that's right. You're going to have a grass band. Try a few common tunes first that everyone knows. It's much like playing the kazoo, except you're using grass.

Bonus video: Here's another simple outdoor thing that can give you hours of fun—rocks. You can explore the underside of rocks and find all kinds of life. Discover more on our video at destinationnature.net.

39: Go Spelunking

ADVENTURE SCALE: 4

The basics: Find yourself a cave to explore. Cave tours are offered in many parts of the country from the karst caves of the Pacific Northwest to the limestone caves of the Ozarks. Find one in your area that offers exploring. To learn if your state has any, go to your state tourism website to start.

Challenge: Some cave tours are wide-open paths that lead in and out. Others are more challenging adventures. Shimmy under a low overhang. Weave in between stalagmites (growing up) and stalactites (growing down).

Did you know: Carlsbad Cavern in New Mexico is one of the most famous caves in the world. You can hike on your own into the cave via Carlsbad Cavern National Park. If you're ever in the area, definitely check it out.

FREEZE 'EM

While canning is a popular option to save your extra harvest, there's even an easier way. Freezing food is fast and fun, and you don't need any experience at all. Here are two options for freezing common foods, along with great recipes.

Freezer Jam Serving Size: 4–6 pint jars
Strawberry jam is probably the most popular to make through freezing, but you can also make freezer jam with many other fruits like blueberries, apricots, and peaches. One of the best things about freezer jam is that it's not a lot of work, so you can make a few (or a lot) of jars in less than an hour. You can usually find recipes for freezer jam in your pectin container, but here's one you can use for either strawberry or peach.

> 2 cups crushed fresh peaches or strawberries
> 4 cups sugar
> 1/8 cup lemon juice
> 1 cup water
> 1 package (1.74-ounce) dry pectin

Mix your fruit, sugar, and lemon juice together in a medium bowl. Let sit. Meanwhile, put the water and pectin in a small saucepan over a medium heat. Once the water mixture barely starts boiling, turn the heat off and carefully add to the fruit mixture. Stir gently by hand for 3 minutes, mixing everything together. You should feel it start to thicken as you stir. Next, pour the mixture into your jars of choice. Use a damp washcloth to clean the edges of the jars and then put lids on tightly. Let the jars sit out at room temperature for about 24 hours. Then put in the freezer. As you're ready to use the jam, remove from the freezer and place in the refrigerator. The jam will be good for a few weeks once you've moved it from the freezer to the refrigerator. Otherwise, it will keep in the freezer up to a year.

You can use bigger or smaller jars as desired. Then consider making up your own personalized stickers to add to your jars. This is a good way to create personalized gifts as well.

Freezer Veggies

You can save your vegetables by freezing them this fall. You can freeze just about any veggie, but those that work best with this technique include beans, corn, carrots, and broccoli. There are three main steps:

1. The first step to getting veggies ready for freezing is to blanch them. Blanching is just a fancy way of saying you boil the veggies for a few minutes. Start the water boiling before you add the veggies. While it can vary, a good rule of thumb is to blanch roughly a pound of veggies in a gallon of water for 2–3 minutes.

2. After the veggies boil for a few minutes, immediately strain them in the sink with cold water. Afterward, it's time to season. Season with your favorite dried herbs. You only need a couple of teaspoons.

3. Now it's time to freeze. Place in gallon freezer bags, making sure you get all the air out before you seal it. You can keep frozen veggies for about a year. When it's time to eat, pull out the veggies, thaw, heat, and serve.

❑ 40: Make Apple Cider
ADVENTURE SCALE: 4

The basics: Many apple orchards offer the chance to help make apple cider, using a large machine or crank to juice the apples. Look for an opportunity like this in your area, and sign up to help. At the least, be sure to pick up a jug of apple cider when you go to an orchard. It really does taste different than apple juice.

Challenge: Try juicing your own apples at home. You're going to need a juicer. You could also try adding them into a blender along with other fruits to make a smoothie. Remember to peel and core the apple first.

Did you know: Many apple orchards sell their products on their website or to local grocery stores during apple season. Some places will even ship entire apple pies to your house. If you can't be there in person, consider this option.

❑ 41: Count the Arms on a Starfish
ADVENTURE SCALE: 2

The basics: While many species of starfish have five arms, some can have more. In fact, lots more! What is the highest number of arms you can find? Did you know that some species of starfish can even grow their arms back if damaged?

Challenge: Have a starfish challenge and see who can spot the most starfish in an hour. Hit the beach and start looking. You're going to find them along the water's edge.

Did you know: Right now, scientists are trying to change the name of the starfish to sea star because it's not actually a fish at all. Starfish are more closely related to sea cucumbers, sea urchins, and sand dollars.

❏ 42: Paddle a Canoe

ADVENTURE SCALE: 4

The basics: Canoes offer plenty of legroom, so they are fairly stable on the water. Canoeing is a two-person activity, and it's a good idea to always take at least two canoes out for safety reasons. Practice getting in and out of the canoe while still on land. The person in the front is the motor of the canoe, while the person in the back is the steering wheel. A third person can sit in the middle of the canoe and enjoy the ride.

Challenge: Go on an overnight canoeing adventure. The Boundary Waters, Okefenokee Swamp, and the Everglades are all classic canoe trip destinations, but you can also find a body of water close to home.

Did you know: Historically people hollowed out logs to use as canoes. Now canoes can be made of wood, plastic, or fiberglass.

❏ 43: Go Rock Climbing

ADVENTURE SCALE: 5

The basics: You can practice on an indoor climbing wall, but you should eventually take it outside to the rocks. Of course, you'll need to make sure you have the right equipment and are being safe. Start off small, and master those steps first before moving on.

Challenge: Don't forget to enjoy the view out there. Take a moment to just relax and take it all in from the top of the rocks. You can stay up there for a few minutes before you rappel down.

Discover more: If you want to get involved in rock climbing and meet others like you, get a parent and check out the website rockclimbing .com. You can also check out your local climbing club or wall to get tips from them.

MOUNTAINS

Hop in the car and head for the mountains. There are numerous mountain drives you can find. While these auto tours offer stunning views and pull-outs for pictures, be sure to venture beyond the pavement too. Mountain destinations offer up numerous opportunities for exploring. From the Appalachian chain to the Tetons, every mountain range tells a unique story. Learn a bit about the local geology to reveal these tales, and then go check them out for yourself.

Who: Whether you'd like to stay at a fancy lodge or spend days hiking in the backcountry, you can find a mountain destination right for you. Mountains are a common destination highlighted by visitor centers, so look for information there or online. You can find something that appeals to you. Don't forget, it's higher elevation than what most of us are used to, so pack plenty of water.

What: Recreation opportunities are boundless in the mountains. While climbing to the top of a mountain can be rewarding, there are plenty of other fun things to explore. For example, try fishing in the mountain streams, hiking through the forests and meadows, or just enjoying a peaceful mountain vista.

When: Fall is a favorite time to visit the mountains, though you can really visit the mountains during every season. (It's fun to compare the differences between seasons.) Visitors flock to the mountains for fall foliage. As the days get shorter and the nights get cooler, the leaves of the deciduous trees change to the bright yellows, oranges, and reds that are synonymous with fall.

Where: North, south, east, and west—there are mountains throughout North America. With an elevation of over 20,000 feet, Mount McKinley (also called Denali) in Alaska is the highest peak on the continent.

Why: The fall mountain air is crisp and refreshing. Grab a light jacket and get out there and enjoy the final days of fall before winter sets in.

Tips and Tricks

Do a little research ahead of time, and it'll really pay off. Find out if there are special events being held, and then visit the mountains around this time. Or if you're pressed for time, look into a local tour service. Many of these services employ local, independent people who just love sharing their area with others. You might even find an organization that offers up volunteers to take you around for free. They'll help you get the most out of your mountain experience.

44: Shoot a Bow

ADVENTURE SCALE: 4

The basics: Bow meets arrow, steady aim at the target, and then release. Archery goes back to medieval times. Still practiced as a means to harvest game, archery is also a growing recreational activity. Offered as a physical education class in some areas, target-shooting leagues can be found in many states. Skip the bowling league this fall, and instead sign up for the archery team.

Challenge: Experiment with shooting both a recurve bow and a more traditional longbow. They require slightly different techniques, and it's an accomplishment to say that you've tried both.

Discover more: Archery was introduced as an Olympic sport in the 1900 games. In 1924, it was discontinued. Then it returned in 1972, and it's still an Olympic sport today.

45: Make Fall Crafts

ADVENTURE SCALE: 3

The basics: Go on a nature hunt and gather interesting objects that you find out and about. Then bring them inside and challenge yourself to create something interesting. Make a collage or turn them into artwork of some kind. Be creative!

Challenge: Have a craft party. More creative minds are better than one. Have your friends bring all kinds of supplies (encourage them to be inventive), and see what you come up with.

Did you know: Craft fairs are popular in fall just before the holidays. This is a great way to buy local and find some unique presents. Look for one (or a few) to attend in your area.

46: Take Leaf Pictures

ADVENTURE SCALE: 2

The basics: Leaves are one of the easiest, yet prettiest, subjects to take pictures of. They are gorgeous, especially on a clear blue-sky day with puffy clouds in the background. Get out and take some pictures, and then turn them into framed art.

Challenge: See how many different colors of leaves and shapes you can capture with your camera, or you can turn it into a leaf picture scavenger hunt. Take two cameras out and see who can capture the most photos of different leaf types in just thirty minutes.

Did you know: Close-up leaf pictures are gorgeous too. After you've gotten your scenic views, arrange some leaves in the backyard for some nice close-ups.

47: Harvest and Roast Pumpkin Seeds

ADVENTURE SCALE: 2

The basics: Pumpkin seeds are easy to harvest and roast. Gather the seeds out of a pumpkin, wash off, and let dry. Then roast in the oven over a low heat (200°F) for two to three hours. Season as desired.

Challenge: Try harvesting sunflower seeds. Even if you didn't grow your own sunflowers, go to a local farmers' market to try to find some heads to buy. Dry, roast, and season just as you'd do pumpkin seeds.

Discover more: Seed Savers Exchange is an organization dedicated to preserving heirloom seeds. They have some cool plants that have been passed down for generations. Learn more at seedsavers.org.

FALL BIRD FEEDERS

Ready to get crafty? This is a great time of year to make your own bird feeder. You don't have to go to the lumber or hardware store either. You can make both of these bird feeders from recycled items that you already have in your house or outside. Make them, and then hang 'em out for your feathered friends or give a couple to a friend.

Log Suet Feeder

Supplies: Log, suet, drill, drill bit, wire, eyehook
Ages: 5 and up
Time: 15 minutes

How-To:

You'll definitely need help from an adult with this one. First find a good-sized log that won't be too heavy when you hang it from a wire. Next, get a drill and a large drill bit. You'll want a big bit, perhaps an inch wide or more, because you're going to put suet in these holes. Mark on your log where you want your holes to be. It works nicely to stagger them. Finally, it's time to drill the holes. Wear protective goggles as an extra precaution. You can either have the hole go all the way through or drill at least 1/2 an inch into the log for each hole. Fill with suet and hang with wire and an eyehook.

Supplies: Plastic plate, drill, wire, silverware, hot glue gun and glue sticks, bird seed

Ages: 6 and up

Time: 20 minutes

How-To:

This is a fun feeder. If you don't have an old plastic plate or silverware around the house, hit up your local thrift shop. You can pick some up for just a few bucks. First off, drill small holes in four different areas of your plate. Think of it like a clock, and mark and drill at the 12, 3, 6, and 9 o'clock positions. Next, thread your wire through, one hole at a time and secure. Leave about 18 inches of wire loose on each section. Then pull those wires together in the center, making sure the plate stays nice and even. Using hot glue, secure a fork and spoon onto the outer rim of the place. This is just for looks—the birds aren't really going to use them. Then hang in a tree and fill with seed.

Tips and Tricks

What else can you recycle to turn into a feeder? Walk around your garage, basement, or a thrift store for a little inspiration. Old baskets, milk jugs, and coffee cans turned on their sides are all viable options. Also grow your own gourds or buy one at the famers' market to turn into a birdhouse.

48: Plant Bulbs

ADVENTURE SCALE: 2

The basics: This is the time to plant bulbs if you want gorgeous tulips, daffodils, and hyacinths next spring. Make sure you get the bulbs in the ground deep enough (follow the directions on the back of the package) and before the ground freezes.

Challenge: Plant at least seven different kinds of bulbs. Yes, there are that many spring bulbs to choose from. Check out your local garden center to check them out. You can mix them all up or try planting them in a neat row. Then see what pops up first in spring.

Bonus video: While you're planting your bulbs, this is also a great time to put in a toad abode (see page 3). Learn how to make a home for your hoppy friends at destinationnature.net.

49: Hold a Pumpkin Carving Party

ADVENTURE SCALE: 3

The basics: It's more fun to carve pumpkins if you do it in a group. Challenge yourself and your partygoers to be creative and carve pumpkins that are beyond ordinary. Be sure to line them up at the end and take a picture of the results.

Challenge: Hold a fun little contest with prizes. You can do a fashion show and have judges or pick the winners via secret ballot. How involved do you want it to be? You could even have music, a talent competition, or more.

Discover more: You can get lots of free pumpkin stencils online. Grab a parent and look for fun pumpkin faces to download. Then trace them onto your pumpkin to create a work of art.

❑ 50: Hug a Tree

ADVENTURE SCALE: 1

The basics: Set this book down right now, go outside, and hug the nearest tree. Even if you've already hugged a tree before, do it again. If you live in a habitat that doesn't have trees, I guess you're off the hook. But the next tree you see, you must hug. No excuses.

Challenge: Keep a life list of all of the different species of trees that you've ever hugged. Better yet, take a picture of yourself hugging all the different trees, and you can keep a picture album.

Did you know: Redwood trees are some of the biggest in the country. They can grow more than three hundred feet high and thirty feet in diameter. This means you'll need a few people joined together to help hug that kind of tree.

ULTIMATE FRISBEE

Fall is football season, which means it's also the perfect time to play Ultimate Frisbee. This game is like of mix of soccer (lots of running) and football (kickoffs and passing). But luckily, you can still use your hands, and there's no tackling involved.

Ages: 7 and up
Materials: Frisbee
Length: 45 minutes (two 20-minute halves and a 5-minute halftime)
Number of players: 6–14

1. To start things off, you need a good field. If you have access to a football field or a soccer field, this is perfect. But if you're just in the backyard, make your own with a designated "goal" area on each end. Keep in mind that you're going to be doing a lot of running, so a bigger field is good. Also, the bigger the field, the more challenging it will be, so if you want to take on a football field, make sure you have older players.
2. Next, you flip a coin or play a quick game of "rock, paper, scissors" to figure out who kicks off first. Once you decide, each team lines up at opposite end zones for kickoff.
3. One person flings the Frisbee as far as he can toward the other team. Everyone runs together, and the other team takes control of the Frisbee first. (The kickoff team cannot run and get the Frisbee. They have to wait for someone on the opposite team to take it first.)
4. In Ultimate Frisbee, you can't actually run with the Frisbee. If you do, that's a penalty. You have to constantly pass it from one player to the next. And one player can't hold it for more than 15 seconds or they'll get a penalty.
5. You also can't tackle players or even touch them for that matter. You can do everything you can to get in front of them and steal the Frisbee away for your team, but no contact. This would be a foul.

6. If a player does hold onto the Frisbee for more than 15 seconds or he runs with it, it goes to the opposite team. If someone commits a foul, the Frisbee either goes to the opposite team or the person who the foul was committed on gets a free pass to an open player.
7. The object of the game is to get the Frisbee down the field and score in your goal. Every time a team scores, there's a new kickoff as well. Keep track of the points, and whoever has the most at the end is deemed the winner.
8. Ultimate Frisbee is usually limited to no more than 7 players per side, or 14 total. If you have more than 14 people who want to participate, you can substitute throughout the game without stopping play.
9. You can have a ref, if you'd like. Otherwise, everyone is on the honor system, and you can all call it as a team (and vote if there are arguments).
10. Don't forget to drink plenty of water and take your 5-minute halftime break. There's a lot of running in this game, so you need to stay hydrated!

WINTER

*"When I no longer thrill to the first snow of the season,
I'll know I'm growing old."*

—LADY BIRD JOHNSON

Winter is definitely the best season. Think about it—it's the ultimate season for embracing all that nature has to offer. Nothing makes you feel more alive than getting outside on a cold crisp day.

Believe it or not, there are so many outstanding winter activities to explore that you could fill an entire year's worth of fun in this season alone. Think about it. You can't snowshoe, ski, or go on a sleigh ride in the summer. And you'll want to experience them all before spring. The only question is—what do you do first?

If you've planned ahead, your garden can remain festive all winter. Ornamental grasses and other perennials left up through winter provide a food source for birds and small mammals. They also add a bit of character to the frozen landscape, and frosty mornings enhance this backyard view.

Animals often gather, feeding together on shared winter range. The chatter of birds is especially encouraging in the winter. These sounds remind us that nature exists all year long.

There is more to winter than snow. Go on a desert adventure for a change of pace. Also, indoor destinations can keep you in touch with nature on the most blustery of days. Visit a greenhouse, and you'll step inside a tropical paradise to leave the wind and cold behind.

After a fresh snow, there is still a freshness in the air. Each step feels like an adventure as you make new tracks in the powder. Back outside, snowball fights and snow angels keep you occupied all winter long. You'll earn your hot chocolate after a full day of snow and fun.

Winter adventure awaits. Just open the door, step outside, and let the fun begin.

Winter's Checklist

1: Make a Snow Angel

ADVENTURE SCALE: 1

The basics: Put on your snow pants, bundle up your coat, tie up your snow boots, and head outside. Plop down on your back and wave your arms and your legs. Yep, it really is that easy!

Challenge: Gather up a bunch of your friends and make a row of snow angels lined up side by side. You can create a whole snow family and even decorate them, just like you'd decorate a snowman.

Did you know: The best time to make a snow angel is right after it snows so the snow is fresh and there aren't tracks to mess up the angel. It's also fun to make a snow angel while it's snowing.

2: Catch a Snowflake on Your Tongue

ADVENTURE SCALE: 2

The basics: This one should be easy. It just takes falling snow and a tongue. So if it starts snowing, head outside and wait. It's magical to watch the snow coming down. See how big of a snowflake you can catch.

Challenge: Rather than catching a snowflake on your tongue, catch one on the tip of your finger. Then quickly examine the shape of the snowflake with a magnifying glass before it melts. If you catch it with a glove on, it might not melt right away.

Discover more: There is actually a field guide to snowflakes. They really are all different. You can learn all about the science of snow at snowcrystals.com.

3: Sketch in Winter
ADVENTURE SCALE: 3

The basics: You know those fingerless gloves you can buy? They make the perfect sketching glove in winter. Take a pad of paper outside and let nature inspire you. Too cold? Sit by the fire and sketch from inside instead. As the snow gently falls, it'll inspire you.

Challenge: Sketch a different thing from nature every day for a week. Make sure it's something different each time. It'll make you look at winter in a whole new way.

Did you know: If you use a waterproof field notebook, you can even sketch when it is snowing outside. Wouldn't it be cool to be sketching while the flakes land on you?

4: Go Ice Fishing
ADVENTURE SCALE: 4

The basics: Make sure the ice is thick and safe. If you go with experienced anglers, they'll know. Ice fishing is great fun. It might take a little more patience than regular fishing, but don't give up.

Challenge: Find an ice hut to fish in (aka, find a friend who has one). It's also called a shanty in some areas. This will keep you protected from the winter winds. Some ice huts are even heated, so you don't have to worry about bundling up too much.

Did you know: Ice conditions vary, but generally clear ice is stronger than cloudy ice. Either way, don't go on the ice unless you know it's definitely thick and strong. Looks can be deceiving.

FUN IN THE SNOW

Whether you live in a place that gets snow regularly or a place that rarely sees it, it's good to be prepared when this fluffy white stuff starts to fall. It's a blast to play with! Here are a couple of snow activities to try—one where you can be artistic and another you can eat. Don't forget to bundle up with snow pants and warm gloves. You'll be glad you did.

Household Snow People

Supplies: Wooden spoons, pipe cleaners, yarn, and anything else you can think of
Ages: 3 and up
Time: 20 minutes

How-To:

1. Go beyond the ordinary carrot nose and twig hands. Use your imagination to create a unique snow boy or snow girl with items from your own house. So after you have your 3 balls rolled and stacked up, start peeking around in drawers and cabinets for things to decorate it with.
2. Start by looking for arms—pipe cleaners, wooden spoons, or anything else that is sturdy and will stick out should work.
3. Next, look for things that will work as eyes and buttons. If you decide to use something flat like real buttons, remember you'll need a good way to attach them. You might be able to use an unrolled paperclip or something similar.
4. The mouth might be the trickiest. If you can't find anything good to use and shape, then think about using snow paint.
5. Finally, don't forget to decorate the top of the head. Add on yarn for hair or borrow one of your hats to place on top. Remember, the most important thing is to have fun. There's no right or wrong way to make your snow person.

Tips and Tricks

You can use a washable paint and paintbrushes for snow paint. Or make your own using a spray bottle, water, and food color. Once you have your snow paint ready, have fun with it. Try playing tic-tac-toe in the snow with paint. You can also create cool art pieces with your paint.

Supplies: Milk, snow, sugar, vanilla, food coloring
Ages: 3 and up
Time: 5 minutes

How-To:

1. Snow ice cream is easy to make, but exact measurements are a bit hard to give. Start off by mixing roughly 10 cups of snow along with 1/2 cup of sugar, 1/2 teaspoon of vanilla, and 1 cup of milk. Stir. Check the consistency and taste. You might want to add more sugar or milk right away.

2. After you have a good consistency, you can add color. Put in a few drops of food coloring and mix. Remember, you only need a few drops.

3. If you want to add in any other flavors, experiment by slicing up fresh fruit to go with your snow ice cream. Fresh bananas, strawberries, or blueberries are all great options. If your ice cream starts to melt, just add some more snow on top. Freshly fallen snow is the best.

Tips and Tricks

You'll want to use fresh clean snow. Try collecting snow off your porch rail or your patio furniture. You can also scrape off the top layer of snow and use the purest snow from the middle of a snowdrift.

5: Build a Snow Fort

ADVENTURE SCALE: 5

The basics: It might take the whole neighborhood to help you build a snow fort, but the effort will be worth it. Go ahead and start gathering friends after a big snowfall. Remember you'll need plenty of air vents, and you'll have to be careful the roof doesn't collapse.

Challenge: Build an igloo. Make snow blocks and then wet them down. Let them freeze overnight and then pile them up to build your very own igloo. If you run out of steam to build an entire igloo, at least build one wall.

Did you know: It's spelled a little different, but the Inuit word *iglu* means "house" no matter what the house is made out of.

6: See a Meteor Shower

ADVENTURE SCALE: 3

The basics: There are plenty of great meteor showers in the winter, including the Leonid, Geminid, and Quadrantid meteor showers. Crisp winter nights can be perfect for viewing the night sky. Grab a warm blanket and a thermos of hot cocoa and head outside.

Challenge: While trying to see meteors, see if you can spot a satellite too. Satellites are bright lights moving steadily across the night sky. It's easier to see them with a telescope, so either use your own or borrow one from a friend.

Did you know: Meteors are tiny bits of interplanetary rock and debris falling through Earth's upper atmosphere, while satellites are objects humans have placed in orbit around the planet.

7: Go Cross-Country Skiing

ADVENTURE SCALE: 5

The basics: Cross-country skiing is some of the best winter exercise around. The skinny skis are a little tricky at first, but with a little practice you'll be kick-gliding along like an Olympic champion. Don't get discouraged if you fall; that is half the fun. You'll get the hang of it eventually.

Challenge: Once you master the basics of cross-country skiing, invite your dog along for the trip. Skijouring is like dog sledding without the sled. Instead you harness up dogs (or sometimes a horse) to pull you along on your skis.

Bonus video: Learn the secret to getting yourself up off the ground without having to take your cross-country skis off at destinationnature .net.

8: Go for a Night Walk in the Snow

ADVENTURE SCALE: 3

The basics: The stillness of the night is especially evident during the winter. If you take a nighttime stroll during a bright moon, the light reflecting off the snow can make it feel like daytime. Keep your eyes peeled to catch a glimpse of nocturnal creatures.

Challenge: Make a list of five different things you want to see at night, and then head out to see them all. It might take you one or two walks on different nights to spot them all, but don't stop until you do.

Did you know: The sun doesn't rise in Barrow, Alaska, for about two months each winter. This makes for a pretty long and dark winter. Be thankful of any sunshine you get in winter.

RED ROVER

Kids have been playing Red Rover outside for years. It's a team game where you form two teams. This is one instance where more people are a good thing. Red Rover teams can be made up of 10 or more per side. Start gathering people up and get a game going.

Ages: 5 and up
Materials: None
Length: 20 minutes
Number of players: 15 or more

1. You need a pretty big open space to play Red Rover. People will be running, so look for a pretty flat area overall. A nice grassy area would be the ideal location.
2. Divide the teams up equally. One group goes to one side and the other group goes to the other side, 50 to 100 feet apart, facing each other.
3. One team goes first. The team gathers around and decides who on the other team they choose to send over. (Example: Maybe they decide to send Julie over.)
4. Once they decide, the group spreads out in a line, holding hands. Then they chant all together: "red rover, red rover, send Julie right over." Julie will try to break through one set of hands, so the team members should be spread out to be fair.
5. At that point, Julie has to leave her group and go running toward the other group. She chooses two people to try to run through to break apart their interlocked hands. She should run fast so she has more momentum to break through.
6. If Julie doesn't break the hands, she must join this new group. But if she does, she gets to choose one person to go back with her to join her group. The group with the most members after several rounds is the winner.

Tips and Tricks

Decide at the beginning of the game how many rounds you want to play (this game could really go on forever). Remind everyone this is a friendly game, so you don't want anyone charging through too hard and hurting anyone.

9: Take a Snowshoeing Hike

ADVENTURE SCALE: 2

The basics: Snowshoeing is as easy as walking. The snowshoes help distribute your weight, so you can walk on top of the snow. It's something everyone should experience at least once.

Challenge: Snowshoe racing generally uses a smaller snowshoe. Have your own race with your friends, or participate in a sanctioned event. Popular distances include five and ten kilometers.

Bonus video: Traditional snowshoes were made with a wooden frame and rawhide webbing. See a comparison of snowshoes at destinationnature.net.

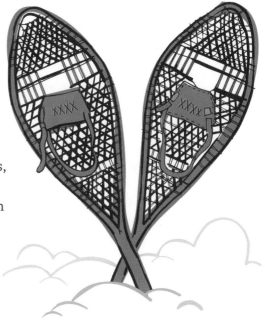

10: Attend a Winter Festival

ADVENTURE SCALE: 2

The basics: Many communities celebrate winter with a festival. Downtowns are transformed with lights, and the cold and snow are celebrated. This is the perfect way to get you outside and enjoying nature, no matter how much you might want winter to be over already.

Challenge: Sign up for an event at the festival. Perhaps you can enter the chili cook-off or be on a team for a sledding race. This is a great way to get involved to make the most of the festival.

Tips and tricks: Use those handy little handwarmer packets to break the chill of a winter day. This will ensure that you can be outside much longer without getting too cold.

11: Dig a Snow Pit and Explore the Layers

ADVENTURE SCALE: 2

The basics: It can be fun to dig a snow pit and explore the different layers of snow. It's neat to see how the snowpack changes throughout the season as layers compress and snow crystals change.

Challenge: Find "sugar snow." Do you know what sugar snow is? It consists of grainy snow crystals that provide a layer of insulation to small mammals that burrow in through the winter.

Did you know: Learning how to dig a snow pit can actually save your life. If you're exploring in an area that is prone to avalanches, you can dig a snow pit to help detect dangerous conditions.

12: Take a Sleigh Ride

ADVENTURE SCALE: 3

The basics: Go on a sleigh ride through a winter wonderland. Sturdy draft horses will pull you along. Unless you know someone with horses and a sleigh, look for a place in your area offering up this opportunity. It's especially popular around the holidays, and you might be able to go see the lights at the same time.

Challenge: Go mushing. Plenty of places offer up dog sledding lessons. You might have to travel to northern parts of the country, though. Hold on tight and feel the wind breeze by your face as the dogs pull you along.

Did you know: Perhaps the most popular sleigh ride is on the National Elk Refuge in northwestern Wyoming. The ride weaves through herds of wintering wildlife including elk and bison.

13: Go Sledding

ADVENTURE SCALE: 2

The basics: You can find a sledding hill just about anywhere. The first dusting of snow gets everyone fired up for the rest of the season. Get your sleds out and ready to go. Then make sure you have a clear path all the way to the bottom of the hill. Ready, set, go!

Challenge: Toboggans are old-fashioned sleds on skis, and you can still find toboggan hills across the country. They are built with ice and can really pick up speed going down the hill. Are you up for the challenge?

Tips and tricks: Ski lodges and other resorts often have hills dedicated to sledding in winter (many waterpark locations will as well). You can rent a tube or a sled for the day, or bring your own.

14: Try Ice Skating

ADVENTURE SCALE: 3

The basics: Whether on a frozen pond, or an indoor rink, ice skating is a fun challenge. Push, glide, push, glide along. Standing on skates can be tricky at first, but soon you'll be ready to try a few fancy moves if you keep practicing.

Challenge: Ditch the skates and play some broomball. Broomball is like hockey, only instead of a stick and a puck you use a broom and a ball. Remember it is all in fun though, so no hip-checking allowed.

Did you know: The earliest ice skates were made by securing animal bones to the bottom of the foot, and then you slid along that way. So if you think ice skating is hard now, just think about how people used to have to do it!

YOUR OWN BACKYARD

Some of the best nature finds ever are right in your own backyard. You might not think your backyard has much to offer, but it does. Nature is everywhere—you just have to look. Of course, the phrase "backyard" means something different to everyone. For those with lots of space, you probably see wildlife and nature every day. But for those who don't, challenge yourself to expand "your own backyard" within a mile or two from your house. There's probably more around than you thought.

Who? Challenge your entire family to discover the backyard together. It doesn't matter how old you are; there's something to see. Sometimes it's the youngest explorers that find the little details that others miss. Make this a regular family experience, though. Go out as an entire group and just look at and appreciate your own backyard.

What? Try a little bit of everything in your backyard—from watching birds and looking for bugs to playing games and just relaxing, you can do it all. Take a weekend and see just how many things you can accomplish in your backyard. With a little creative planning, you can do a lot.

When? It's good to keep a journal of what you can find in your backyard during every season, but winter is an especially good time to check it out. Here's why—you might think winter is cold and inactive, but it's not. You'll have to search a little harder, but bundle up and check things out. Perhaps you'll find animal tracks in the snow. Maybe different birds will visit your feeders in the winter.

Where? After you've explored your immediate backyard, start expanding. What's within a mile of your house that you can check out? What's within 5 miles? While they aren't immediately right outside your back door, it's pretty cool to say it's in your neighborhood.

Why? Sometimes we get so focused on going to destinations that we forget about the things that are right at our fingertips. Don't overlook these. It's easy to go somewhere and spend money to be entertained. But the backyard offers free enjoyment, and you don't have to get in a car to go.

Tips and Tricks

Rather than planning a vacation, try a staycation. You'll have a new appreciation of where you live if you treat your hometown as a destination. There are bound to be places you've yet to explore in your own area. Make a list of places you want to check out in your neighborhood, and then start checking them off the list.

15: Build a Snowman

ADVENTURE SCALE: 2

The basics: Make yourself a classic snowman and a snowwoman. Use extra clothes or other household items to help you decorate your snow people. Be sure to give your snow people hats, scarves, and complete faces. Then break out the camera and take a picture of your creations.

Challenge: Why limit yourself to a snowman and snowwoman? What other snow sculptures can you create? How about a snow duck or a snow deer? Perhaps you could create a whole snow family, complete with a dog and cat.

Did you know: If you have light snow that isn't packing well, add a little bit of water to it to help pack it in even better. You don't need much. Use a spray bottle or just a few sprinkles.

16: Feed a Bird Up Close

ADVENTURE SCALE: 3

The basics: When it's cold, birds will often come in close to feed. Sit out by your feeder area with the feeder in your lap or in your hand. Then wait for the birds to come up and eat. You'll love this up-close look at birds. Remember, you're going to have to be patient for this to work, so bundle up. You could be sitting there for a little while.

Challenge: Chickadees are fairly easy birds to attract up close, so challenge yourself to attract two or three other species while you're out there. You might even be able to get a squirrel to pay you a visit.

Tips and tricks: Feed the birds at about the same time each day. This will help establish a routine for you and the birds. So when the feeder is empty and you come out to fill it, they'll be ready. Hopefully they'll be feeding out of your hand in no time!

17: Plant an Indoor Garden

ADVENTURE SCALE: 3

The basics: Gardening can be a year-round activity, even in the cold North. You just have to plant an indoor garden. Herbs make great indoor garden projects. Or try starting your own terrarium. Hit up your garden center and see what they have for indoor plants as well. They might have some cool varieties that you never knew about.

Challenge: Force bulbs inside. Forcing bulbs simply means making them bloom when you want them to. Try forcing tulips, daffodils, or other spring bulbs indoors. The bulbs will need a cold period before you plant them. Try storing them in the garage or even the refrigerator before forcing them.

Bonus video: Want a few tips for forcing bulbs indoors? You can learn more and get tips for guaranteed success by watching our video at destinationnature.net.

18: Go Animal Tracking

ADVENTURE SCALE: 3

The basics: Winter is a great time for finding animal tracks. You can follow the path through the snow. What was the animal doing? Searching for food? Running quickly away from a predator? Don't just think of traditional prints, though. It is especially neat to see wing prints in the snow as a bird flies away.

Challenge: Find some scat. Animal scat is the science term for poop. (Isn't it cool to be able to tell your friends you know a word for poop?) You can often tell what species of animals are in an area simply by looking for their scats. If you follow animal tracks long enough you'll be able to find some scat.

Did you know: Some species mark their territory with scat. Also you can sometimes tell what an animal has been eating if you look at the scat really close. You're just like a scientist now.

NUTS

Nuts are one of the most popular gifts around the holidays. Here's the perfect gift—give someone a bag of nuts, a nutcracker, and a recipe to make her own unique mix. Here, you'll find both a sweet and spicy recipe. You can use any nuts to make these, so try out a few and see what you like best.

Sweet and Tasty Nuts Serving size: 6

1 1/2 cups sugar
1/4 teaspoon salt
1 teaspoon cinnamon
6 tablespoons milk
1/2 teaspoon vanilla
1 1/2 cups nuts (pecans, cashews, peanuts, etc.)

Mix the first four ingredients and cook slowly until the sugar dissolves. Increase the heat slightly and cook until it forms a soft ball. Stir occasionally. Remove from the heat, then add vanilla and nuts. Beat until the mixture thickens and hardens. Turn onto wax paper and quickly separate with a fork.

Spicy and Salty Nuts Serving size: 6

1 1/2 cups nuts (pecans, cashews, peanuts, etc.)
2 tablespoons butter, melted
1 tablespoon sugar
1 teaspoon cumin
3/4 teaspoon chili powder
1/4 teaspoon red pepper
1 teaspoon salt

Toss the nuts in melted butter. Combine all the other ingredients and sprinkle evenly over the nuts, tossing to coat. Spread the nuts in a single layer on a baking sheet. Bake at 325°F for 15 minutes, stirring halfway through cook time.

Tips and Tricks
Check out your seasoning aisle in the grocery store (or go to a specialty shop— that's always fun). Mix your favorite seasoning with nuts and a little bit of salt. Toss to coat and enjoy your own favorite mix!

19: Go on a Conifer Search

ADVENTURE SCALE: 2

The basics: Winter is a good time to
search for pines, spruces, firs, and other
evergreens (also called conifers).
Many people call all of these trees the
same thing, but they're actually
very different. In fact, there are
hundreds of different kinds.
See if you can pick out the
differences by looking at the
height of the tree, shape of
the needles, and so on.

Challenge: Look for different
cones on the conifers. These
are also a good indicator of different
types of trees. Go for a walk either in your backyard or at a local park
and see if you can spot five different kinds.

Tips and tricks: Try to roll the needles between your fingers and
thumb. Pine has round needles, fir has flat needles, and spruce has
square needles.

20: Go Downhill Skiing

ADVENTURE SCALE: 5

The basics: The speed and excitement of downhill skiing is tough to
beat. Most places with snow have several ski options. You can get a les-
son from a ski instructor, and then begin on the bunny slopes. Before
you know it, you'll be hitting the big hills.

Challenge: Snowboarding is becoming more and more popular. It is a
bit like surfing or skateboarding down a snow-covered hill. Start practicing and see if you can master this sport.

Did you know: Olympic downhill skiers can reach speeds of more than
ninety miles per hour. This is faster than cars are allowed to go on the
highway.

21: Make a Winter Bird Feast

ADVENTURE SCALE: 2

The basics: You can use inspiration from our DIY wreaths project in this chapter (see page 168) to start off with, but don't stop there. Put out seed, suet, fruit, fresh water, and several other food offerings for your birds. Then see who shows up for dinner. (A lot of people put out their old Christmas tree after the holidays to make a bird feast area.)

Challenge: Set a goal of how many different types of birds you want to attract to your feast in a single day. Twenty is a good starter goal. If you don't meet it, try again the next day or week. And if you hit it, increase your goal.

Discover more: Project FeederWatch is a winter citizen science project of the Cornell Lab of Ornithology. It is fun and easy to participate in your own backyard. Learn more about it at birds.cornell.edu/pfw/.

22: Look for Winter Berries

ADVENTURE SCALE: 2

The basics: Many plants, like juniper, chokecherry, and holly keep berries all winter long. These can provide essential food for birds. Gather them up and hang them up around your feeders to bring in birds. This is a great activity to add to the bird feast.

Challenge: With a little patience and a few tips from our DIY wreaths project (see page 168), you can make a whole wreath out of berry vines. It'll be pretty, too. Don't worry if you mess up—just keep working and reworking it until you have it the way you want.

Did you know: Many garden centers sell berry vines by the bundle. Buy some to add to your wreath project. Or if you have a neighbor or friend that has berries, ask if they'd like to share.

DIY WREATHS

Nothing says winter and the holidays like a wreath, and it's even more satisfying when you can make your own. It's not as hard as you might think. Don't worry about it being perfect—just give it your best shot and hang with pride. You'll love being able to tell people that you made it yourself.

Evergreen Wreath

Supplies: Wire hanger, evergreen branches, twine, berries, red bow
Ages: 5 and up
Time: 15 minutes

How-To:

1. Bend your wire hanger until it's a large round shape. By using a hanger, you'll have a nice built-in hook too.
2. Look for long evergreen branches. If you don't have any yourself, you can also buy some long boughs at your local garden store. They sell them around the holidays for decoration.
3. Wrap the evergreens around the hanger, securing with twine as needed. For best results, you'll want to wrap the hanger several times to cover it fully and completely.
4. Tuck branches with berries in the evergreen, securing them one at a time. This will add great color to your wreath and will also attract birds.
5. Add a red bow to the top of your wreath. It looks great, and it will also help hide the hook of the hanger.

Grapevine Wreath

Supplies: Grapevine or other woody vine, twine, birdseed ornament
Ages: 7 and up
Time: 20 minutes

How-To:

1. Working with grapevine or other woody vines takes a little practice, but if you can master it, you can make some cool wreaths. Start shaping your wreath using a thicker, sturdier section of the vine. Tie it together tightly at the top.
2. Continue wrapping the wreath in layers of vine, using twine to secure when necessary. You'll want to create several layers of vine for the best look. Remember that no two wreaths will be alike. The best part about working with vine is you get a unique look each time. Often, the wreath will take a shape and life of its own.
3. At the top of the wreath, make a large loop. This will be used to hang your wreath.
4. Finally, get one of those decorative birdseed ornaments you see at the store. They're often in the shape of bells or stars around the holidays. Hang one in the center of your wreath, and put it out in a tree to feed the birds.

Tips and Tricks

Wreaths make a great place to attract birds. You already know you can add berries and birdseed ornaments to wreaths, but don't stop there. String popcorn and cranberries to hang on your wreath too. Attach fresh fruit slices like orange or apples. You can even attach little bowls with wire and place seed or suet inside. Also, who says wreaths have to be round? Try shaping your wreath into a square, star, or triangle.

23: Find Winter Waterfowl

ADVENTURE SCALE: 3

The basics: Ducks, geese, and swans are some of the most visible birds in the winter. As long as the water isn't frozen (and sometimes even when it is), you can find these birds on ponds, lakes, rivers, and oceans. Also look for waterfowl eating out in the farm fields.

Challenge: Find a group of birds wintering together. Swans, for example, are notorious for grouping up during the winter months. Ask area nature centers or birders for tips on where to find them. Once you know where to look, it's pretty easy to spot them.

Did you know: So how do these water birds swim in freezing cold water? Plenty of warm down feathers and special adaptations in their legs keep waterfowl warm in extreme conditions.

24: Put Out a Birdbath

ADVENTURE SCALE: 2

The basics: Not only will birds bathe in the birdbath, they'll also drink up the water. They will love having a fresh water source since most water in winter is frozen. If it's especially cold out, you might have to melt the water a few times a day so the birds can still get at it.

Challenge: Add a heater to your birdbath. You'll have to invest a little bit of money in this, but then you don't have to worry about melting the ice all the time.

Tips and tricks: Flowing water will help keep the birdbath from freezing and will also attract more birds. This is a trick for bringing in more birds year-round. Birds are attracted to things they can hear.

25: Turn Water into Ice

ADVENTURE SCALE: 2

The basics: Here's a fun experiment in winter—see how long it takes to freeze water into ice. Try different areas of your backyard to see if it makes a difference. Can you think of ways to make it freeze faster or slower?

Challenge: On a really cold day, you can toss a glass of water up in the air and it will freeze before it hits the ground. At least that's what certain science experiments say. Bundle up and try it!

Did you know: Water freezes at 0° Celsius or at 32° Fahrenheit. It can be fun to use a thermometer to track how cold the water is. Observe it very closely at the exact moment it starts to freeze or then melt.

26: See the Northern Lights

ADVENTURE SCALE: 4

The basics: The northern lights are one of nature's finest sights. While they're easier to see the farther north you are, even southern residents can see the northern lights on occasion. Winter is one of the best times to see them, so go out there and take a look on a clear night.

Challenge: Get a great photograph of the northern lights. You might have to play with the settings on your camera a little bit to get a good night shot. It looks like magic in the sky, and it's amazing to capture it on camera.

Discover more: The Geophysical Institute at the University of Alaska Fairbanks provides aurora forecasts. See if you'll have a chance to experience the northern lights tonight by going to gi.alaska.edu.

BUNS, BISCUITS, AND BREADS

Spend a Sunday afternoon in the kitchen making your favorite buns, biscuits, or bread. Whatever you make, it'll go great with the soup you make after being outside. Here are three favorite recipes from Stacy's family. They've been passed down for generations.

Yellow Buns Serving size: 12

> 1 1/2 cups milk
> 1/2 cup cornmeal
> 3 teaspoons yeast (1 package)
> 1/2 cup warm water
> 4 cups flour
> 1/2 cup butter
> 1/2 cup sugar
> 2 eggs
> 1 teaspoon salt

Scald the milk. Mix the cornmeal into the scalded milk. Let sit 10 minutes. Dissolve the yeast in warm water. Add 2 cups flour, butter, sugar, eggs, and salt. Stir in cornmeal/milk mixture. Knead. Stir in enough flour to make soft dough, about 2 more cups. Knead until smooth and elastic on a floured surface. Place the dough in a greased bowl and cover with plastic wrap. Place the bowl in a warm draft-free location and allow the dough to rise to double in bulk. Punch the dough down. Shape into 2 1/2-inch balls and place in a greased cooking pan. Allow to rise to double in bulk. Bake at 400°F for about 18 to 20 minutes.

Easy Buttermilk Biscuits Serving size: 10

1 1/2 cups flour

1 tablespoon baking powder

1/2 teaspoon soda

1/2 stick butter

3/4 cup buttermilk

Combine the flour, baking powder, and soda. Melt the butter in the pan you use to bake the biscuits. Rotate the pan to cover the bottom and sides. Pour the excess butter in the biscuit batter. Add the buttermilk. Stir just until dry ingredients are coated. Turn out on slightly floured board. Shape and pat dough to form a pancake shape, 1/2-inch thick. Cut with a floured biscuit cutter (the ring of a jar works well too). Bake in an iron skillet (or pan of your choice) at 400°F for 12–15 minutes.

Banana Bread Serving size: 20

1 cup brown sugar

1 cup white sugar

1 cup oil

4 eggs, well beaten

2 cups flour

1 teaspoon salt

2 teaspoons baking soda

4-6 bananas, mashed

Cream the sugars and oil. Add the eggs, flour, salt, and soda. Mix well. Slowly add the bananas. Spray the loaf pan (one bigger one or two smaller ones) with a non-stick cooking spray and pour the mixture inside. Bake at 350°F for an hour to an hour and a half. Don't open the oven for the first hour because it could affect the rising bread. If you like nuts or chocolate chips, try adding those to your banana bread just to mix it up.

Tips and Tricks

Look for Stacy's family cornbread recipe and Ken's family dinner roll recipe at destinationnature.net.

27: Enjoy a Sunny Winter Day

ADVENTURE SCALE: 1

The basics: Every winter, there are a few rare days where it feels like spring. The sun is shining, the temperatures are high, and you just want to go outside and enjoy the day. Whenever you have a day like this, seize it. Chances are, it's going to get cold again, so you have to enjoy any sunshine you can get.

Challenge: Explore two different parks on one of these sunny winter days. It might still be a bit chilly out, so bundle up, but then go out exploring.

Discover more: Mount Washington in New Hampshire has some of the worst weather in the world. You can follow along at mountwashington.org to see how extreme the weather can be all winter long.

28: Make Indoor S'mores

ADVENTURE SCALE: 2

The basics: You don't have to wait for summer to make s'mores. Roast your marshmallows over your fireplace and you can still get the crackle of the fire. If you don't have an indoor fireplace, you could even use the top of a stove burner. Make this campfire favorite with the whole family.

Challenge: Have a taste-testing contest to see who can roast the most perfect marshmallow. You should make the test blind so people don't cheat and just vote for their own. Or you could have judges who do the tasting and voting.

Tips and tricks: Use a peanut butter cup instead of chocolate for a twist on this traditional favorite. What else can you think of you want to try?

20 QUESTIONS

The game 20 Questions is a great game because you can play it almost anywhere. You can play it while you're out looking for birds. You can play it on the road while on the way to the lake. You can play it while you're out on the canoe. It's really one of the most versatile games out there. Best of all, anyone can play.

Ages: 3 and up
Materials: None
Length: 5–10 minutes for each game
Number of players: 2 or more

1. Pick someone to go first. Then think of something in nature. It can be anything—an animal, an object, etc. Try to pick something that will take players lots of questions to figure out. So just picking a bear is okay, but challenge yourself to think of something a bit harder.
2. The other players in the game start to ask questions about what the item is. (For example: Is it an animal? Does it live in the wild? Does it have fur?) Everyone should take turns asking questions so it's not the same person asking the questions.
3. The person who is "it" must answer the questions truthfully and keep count of how many questions are asked.
4. Choose your questions carefully! You only get 20. After you hit 20, the it person can either reveal what her item was or she can give some good clues so the guessing can continue. Whoever guesses the item correctly gets to be the person to go next.

Tips and Tricks

If you're trying to guess what the item is, work together as a team. You all have to share the questions, so you might as well share ideas. Make sure you agree on the specific questions to ask to give you the best chance for guessing the item. If younger players need help, have them team up with an older child or adult.

29: Try a Winter Sport

ADVENTURE SCALE: 3

The basics: Hockey is one of the most popular sports on ice, but keep in mind that you have to be a pretty good skater. You can also turn an ordinary winter sport like kickball into a winter version. Just use your imagination and find a way to get outdoors and moving this winter.

Challenge: Try curling outside. It's a winter Olympic sport that involves big heavy stones and throwing them across ice. You find clubs that play both inside and out, and they usually welcome newbies. Give it a try at least once.

Did you know: Made of granite, each curling stone weighs approximately forty-two pounds. People also use special shoes so they can slide on the ice when they throw the stone.

30: Take Winter Nature Photos

ADVENTURE SCALE: 2

The basics: Snow and ice are both gorgeous. And best of all, they don't move much, so it's easy to capture great winter photos. Look for a day when the sun is out, because it'll really make the snow and ice sparkle.

Challenge: Capture a picture of a bird at a feeder. You can set up in a window inside so you don't get too cold. Then open the window and snap a shot when the birds stop by for a treat.

Tips and tricks: Snow makes the landscape brighter. Be careful not to overexpose your photos. Even on automatic digital cameras, take a look at the photos right after you take them to make sure they look good.

31: Go to the Desert

ADVENTURE SCALE: 3

The basics: Plenty of snowbirds head south to live for the winter. You don't have to move to the desert each winter, but you should make a winter visit to the desert at least once. You're bound to discover new things, and it's always a good experience to test out a new climate.

Challenge: Go for a desert hike. Be sure to pack plenty of water, though. The temperature might not be too hot, but most people aren't used to the dry air. It really dehydrates your body.

Did you know: Saguaro cactus, found in the Sonoran Desert of Arizona, is the largest cactus in the United States. Saguaro can be up to sixty feet tall and weigh between 3,200 and 4,800 pounds. It is estimated that they can live two hundred years.

32: Have a Winter Cookout

ADVENTURE SCALE: 2

The basics: Yes, it's winter. And no, most people don't cook out in winter. But don't let that stop you. Dust the snow off of your grill and fire it up. Mmm! It's a good way to have a little piece of summer even when it's cold outside.

Challenge: What other summer traditions can you repeat in winter? Make other summer food like strawberry shortcake or a smoothie to continue the summer-in-winter celebration.

Did you know: If you have a charcoal grill, you can just build a fire with wood in it to grill over. It's a fun alternative to traditional grilling.

HANDPRINT MOSAICS

Handprint art is one of the most classic, beloved gifts of all time. Every mother, father, and grandparent will love it. Best of all, you don't have to spend a lot of money. Since you already have the most important part of making this gift—a hand—it's going to be a cinch. Plus, it'll make the perfect present for the holidays!

Supplies: Plate or tray, pencil, glue, beans
Ages: 3 and up
Time: 20 minutes

How-To:

1. Look for the perfect plate or tray to make your handprint on. You can use an old one you have or look at a thrift store or garage sale to see if you can pick one up for less than $1. You don't have to stick to plates or trays either. You might also use the bottom of a terra cotta pot or a large picture frame.
2. Once you choose what your handprint will go on, trace your hand with a pencil, pressing lightly.
3. Using a strong glue that will dry clear, apply it on your handprint in small sections. You want to do it a little bit at a time so it doesn't dry before you're ready to apply your mosaic.
4. Now it's time to apply your beans. Place them one at a time onto the glue. Press gently. Work in small sections, filling each one out completely before moving to the next. This is where you can have a little bit of fun with color and what you place where. Look at the mosaic overall. If you make a mistake or want to move something around, now is the time.
5. If you want to add on a message or date with mosaics, use your finger to write it out in glue first. Then line each letter with your beans, spelling out your message.

6. Once you have your handprint filled up, let it dry for at least 24 hours.

7. After it's dry, check to make sure everything is stuck down. If needed, glue down some of the loose items. You can make several of these for very little money. It's also a great project to do with a small group or class.

More Mosaic Nature Ideas
Small pieces of bark
Pebbles
Dried flower petals
Twigs
Seeds

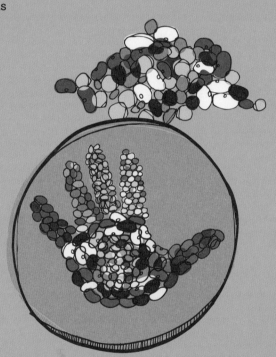

Tips and Tricks
Look for a tray or something large where you can make mosaics with several handprints. Or try making mosaic handprints on a terra cotta pot or other garden item that will make a good gift.

33: Use a Sundial

ADVENTURE SCALE: 2

The basics: A sundial is a little tool used to track sunlight and tell what time it is. See if you can master how to read one. If you can't find one, see if a local nature center or museum has one to try.

Challenge: Learn how to read the sun and tell time by where it's positioned in the sky and without using any tools at all. You might need to use a watch at first, but then eventually you'll learn how to tell time solely by the way the sun is positioned.

Did you know: Even before sundials, people tracked time by measuring an object's shadow. For instance, they would look at where a rock's shadow was and predict what time of day it was.

34: On a Sunny Day, Listen for Birds

ADVENTURE SCALE: 1

The basics: A lot of people think birds only sing and make noise in spring, but this isn't the case at all. Go outside in winter when a sunny day hits, and the birds will be out, celebrating the warmth with the rest of us.

Challenge: Learn how to whistle a bird song yourself. If done in the right way, you just might be able to attract a bird. Or a bird might hear you and decide to sing back at you.

Did you know: A few birds have winter themes in their names. Have you ever seen a snow bunting or a winter wren? How about a snowy owl? Look them up in your field guide. If they are in your area, see if you can spot one.

35: Make an Ice Sculpture

ADVENTURE SCALE: 4

The basics: Start with a block of ice. Then start chipping away at it a little at a time to shape it. If you have a winter festival in your area, check out some of the pros—they really know what they're doing.

Challenge: Make a good ice sculpture. Yep, anyone can make an ice sculpture, but it takes some real talent to make a good one. Practice, practice, practice. And get some additional tips from watching some pros.

Did you know: Colorado hosts the International Snow Sculpture Championships each winter. If there's even a chance you're going to be in the area, it's worth checking out.

36: Have a Snowball Fight

ADVENTURE SCALE: 2

The basics: Pack up a ball of snow and toss it at your friends. What could be better than a friendly snowball fight? Watch your back, though. They'll be firing snowballs back at you just as fast as they can make them.

Challenge: Have a snowball shot-put contest. Make large snow-balls and see who can toss them the farthest. Make sure everyone stands in the same spot for throwing. Then mark each snowball so you know who threw it.

Did you know: This is where you'll watch to use your trick about packing snowballs again. Use a little bit of water to pack them tight. They'll be better for throwing and will stay together a lot longer.

LOCAL, STATE, AND NATIONAL WILDLIFE REFUGES

You're never far from a great adventure when it comes to the National Wildlife Refuge System. Today, there are more than 500 refuges all across the country, and they do a great job of preserving our plants, wildlife, birds, and more. All together, these refuges cover more than 150 million acres (that's bigger than the whole state of California), yet many people don't even realize they exist. National Wildlife Refuge land is protected so people can't build on it or develop it. And since the government owns it, you technically own part of it too. The phrase from the famous Woody Guthrie song, "this land is your land; this land is my land" certainly rings true for refuges. Get out there and enjoy!

Who? Refuges are for the entire family. Most have great paths even for strollers. Or, for older kids, check out the biking trails or the hiking along refuge trails that are a little less traveled. You will also find that many locations have auto tours as well, which is a great way to cover a lot of ground in a short amount of time. Best of all, refuge activities are usually free or are very inexpensive for families, so you don't have to worry about spending a lot to have a fun day out.

What? First off, refuges are a great place to find native plants, insects, and wildlife. Take a magnifying glass, camera, and/or binoculars. You can do a variety of activities at refuges, including hiking, fishing, bird watching, and more. Many refuges even have special activities or programs throughout the year. So get in touch with your local refuges, check out their visitor centers, and support them and their local programming.

When? While you can go to refuges year-round, many people overlook going in winter. Don't make that mistake! Pick a sunny day, bundle up, and head out to explore. You don't have to go out for long or for very far, but winter is one of the most peaceful times to visit. Plus, you'll see plenty of animals out looking for food. To learn about events in winter and beyond, sign up for their newsletters or get on their e-mail list. Then they can stay in touch and keep you informed.

Where? They're everywhere. Go online to www.fws.gov/refuges and you can search for refuges by state or using your zip code. Most states have several to choose from, so chances are, there's one just a short drive away. Remember: refuges are in areas that often have marshes, are on water, or are off the beaten path. So even if you have to go a little out of your way, it's worth it.

Why? It's hard to find a better setting that's so close to home and celebrates your area's best features. The job of refuges is to preserve the land around us, so it's like seeing your own backyard in all of its natural glory. In addition, many of the people that work at refuges are volunteers. So get out and support these local programs. It helps ensure that they'll be around for generations to come.

Tips and Tricks
Duck Stamps will get you free admission into National Wildlife Refuges. Learn more at www.duckstamp.com.

Did You Know?
President Theodore Roosevelt and the US Fish and Wildlife Service helped get this program started way back in 1903. Roosevelt saw the importance of preserving America's most valuable natural land, and he named Florida's Pelican Island as the first official refuge.

37: Go to a Butterfly House

ADVENTURE SCALE: 2

The basics: Indoor butterfly houses are the perfect spot to visit in winter. The butterflies will make you think it's summer. You can check out a butterfly book at the library to learn more about these amazing fliers.

Challenge: Get a butterfly to land on you. To give yourself a better shot, wear bright colors so they'll think you're a flower. But above all, you have to be patient. If you wait long enough and don't move around too much, you'll get one to land sooner or later.

Did you know: Mourning cloak butterflies will overwinter as adults in the wild, and can become active in late winter and early spring.

38: Whittle a Branch

ADVENTURE SCALE: 4

The basics: Whittling is a fancy way to say carving. Yes—it does involve using a knife, so this activity is best saved for older kids with the supervision of an adult. But give this classic hobby a try.

Challenge: Whittle a shape. Creating wood art takes a lot of patience and a special touch. Start off simple by whittling a duck or snake. Also, remember that it doesn't happen instantly. It'll take a little time.

Discover more: There are carving clubs everywhere. These clubs are always eager to share their passion with beginners, so see if you can find one in your area.

39: Grow an Avocado Pit

ADVENTURE SCALE: 2

The basics: Save the pit of an avocado. Then stick toothpicks in either side and set it on top of a jar filled with water. Be sure to keep water filled to the top of the jar. Pretty soon, you should see your pit start to sprout roots. Keep the water filled up to the top of the jar for best results.

Challenge: Once you have several roots going, see if you can pot your pit and grow it into a plant. This is going to be a challenge—give it lots of sunshine—but it's worth a shot.

Did you know: The vast majority of the avocados produced in the United States are grown in Southern California. Also, avocados are the major ingredient in guacamole.

40: Milk a Cow

ADVENTURE SCALE: 3

The basics: Everyone should milk a cow at least once. You're going to need to find a farm that allows you to milk their cows, so look around. (Of if you know someone with a milking cow, that's even better.) Make sure you have someone that knows what they're doing show you how it's done. There is a technique involved.

Challenge: Visit a dairy farm to get an even better look at where milk comes from. Most dairy farms allow you to visit. It's impressive to see how much milk is produced in just one place.

Did you know: Holstein cattle, the black and white ones, are just one of the numerous breeds that are used in dairy production. Other breeds include Guernsey, Jersey, and Brown Swiss.

SIMON SAYS

Simon Says is a pretty simple game if you think about it. All you have to do is follow along and do exactly what you're told. Don't get too confident, though. It really is a lot harder than it sounds. Play this game with just a couple of people or play it with a big group of 20. Either way, it's a great game, and you can play it just about anywhere.

Ages: 3 and up
Materials: Plate or tray, pencil, glue, beans
Length: 15 minutes
Number of players: 2 or more

1. Simon Says is basically a game of copycat, so if you can just copy someone, you should be able to do pretty well. You have to do whatever Simon tells you to do. To get the game started, pick someone to be Simon. It's best if this person has played before and knows how the game works. He can help explain it to some of the new people.
2. Simon must start every command with the words, "Simon says." (Example: Simon says to touch your toes. Simon says to hop on one foot. Simon says to do 5 jumping jacks.) Everyone must follow along to whatever Simon demands, and they must do the task until Simon tells them to stop. (Example: Simon says you can stop hopping on 1 foot.) Of course, if Simon tells you to do 5 jumping jacks, you can stop after 5. But if Simon tells you to pat your head, you better not stop patting until Simon says.
3. Here's the thing, though. Simon can be very tricky. He will try to give you a command without first saying "Simon says." So if he does, and you follow along, you've been tricked and you're out of the game.

4. Remember, this is a listening game more than anything. Listen very carefully and only pay attention to commands that start with "Simon says." Everything else is probably a trick, so just ignore it. If you can follow along exactly and be the last person standing at the end, you could be the winner.

Tips and Tricks

When you are Simon, here's a good way to trick people—do the actions with them. Most people get used to following along, so if you are doing the commands with the other players, give a command that doesn't say "Simon says" first—they'll be less likely to notice if you're doing it with them.

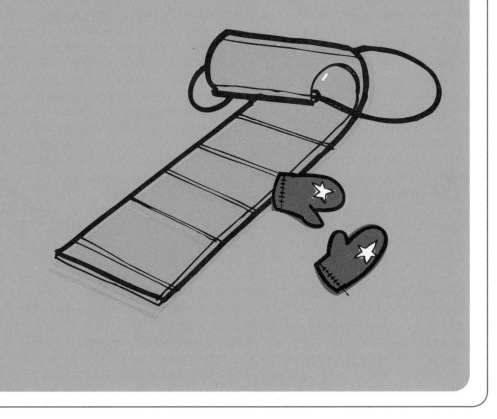

41: Eat an Icicle

ADVENTURE SCALE: 2

The basics: Grab an icicle and give it a lick. You'll want to be careful when you remove the hanging icicles (they can fall and be quite sharp). Don't forget to have gloves on so your fingers don't freeze.

Challenge: Make your own Popsicle with the icicle. You can wet it and then roll it in sugar or dip it in another flavor. You could even add a bit of food coloring to give it a little flavor.

Did you know: Gloves have fingers, so they are helpful for grabbing things. Mittens can keep your hands even warmer. Or you can try the lobster style for the best of both worlds.

42: Write a Nature Haiku

ADVENTURE SCALE: 3

The basics: Haiku are poems that contain three lines. The first line contains five syllables, the second line contains seven syllables, and the final line contains five syllables. Let nature inspire you and write something.

Challenge: Write a new haiku every day for a week. Find something about nature and winter to write about every day. No two poems can be alike—so don't write about snow twice. Be imaginative!

Did you know: Haiku is a traditional form of Japanese poetry that usually has a focus on nature. Be sure to take part in this historical pastime.

43: Play on the Playground after a Fresh Snow
ADVENTURE SCALE: 2

The basics: The best part about going to the playground in winter is that you'll probably have the whole thing to yourself. Put your snow boots on and get out there to enjoy everything you'd do in summer too.

Challenge: Build a big snow pile at the bottom of the slide. Then when you zoom down, you can crash into the snow. After one person crashes through, build it back up again for the next person.

Tips and tricks: You can find battery-operated socks with tiny heaters to keep your toes warm. If that's a little too high tech for you, look for toe warmers.

44: Have a Winter Fire
ADVENTURE SCALE: 2

The basics: Break the winter chill with a warm fire. Now you'll have to huddle in close, and you might want to rotate yourself on occasion from front to back. But there's nothing like a roaring fire right in the midst of the cold.

Challenge: Cook dinner on your fire. Want to roast some marshmallows, make s'mores, or even roast some hot dogs? Don't let the cold stop you! Get out your supplies and get cooking.

Did you know: It can be difficult to get a fire going in winter. Be sure to use some kindling (small sticks and pieces of wood) to help get it going early on, and be sure to have adult supervision.

SOUPS

When it's a bit chilly outside, nothing soothes you like soup. Put on a pot of soup and let it simmer for the afternoon or throw everything into a slow cooker and you can let it go all day. Then use it as an excuse to go outside and explore. Knowing that you have a nice bowl of warm soup waiting for you will help you power through. Here are two recipes to keep you going this winter. One is for a traditional vegetable beef soup, which you can adjust according to what you like. The other is a homemade noodle recipe, which is a great addition to any soup.

Vegetable Beef Soup Serving size: 10

> *6 cups water*
> *2 bay leaves*
> *1 1/2 pounds beef stew meat*
> *1 large can tomato juice*
> *1 onion, chopped*
> *2 teaspoons Worcestershire sauce*
> *1/4 teaspoon chili powder*
> *5 potatoes, cubed*
> *1 bunch celery, chopped*
> *1 large can diced tomatoes*
> *1 bag frozen carrots, lima beans, or mix*

Bring the water, bay leaves, stew meat, tomato juice, and onions together on a low heat for 2–3 hours. Next, remove the bay leaves and break up the meat. Add the rest of the ingredients and bring together on a low heat for another 2–3 hours. Serve when veggies are tender.

Homemade Noodles Serving size: 6

4 eggs
1/4 cup milk
2 cups flour
1 teaspoon salt

Whisk together the eggs and milk. Add 1 cup flour and salt. Stir well. Add the remaining flour until the mixture is not sticky. Roll out on a heavily floured surface. Gently knead. Roll out to 1/4-inch thick. Cut in desired width (probably 1/4 to 1/2 inch). Drop a few at a time into boiling water or chicken broth. Gently stir. Continue until all noodles are added. Cook until tender— this should only take a few minutes. Add the noodles to your favorite soup to make it even more filling.

Tips and Tricks
Here's an easy way to make a quick meal out of noodles—add some chicken broth and then a can of shredded chicken or tuna. It's quick and delicious.

❏ 45: Put Up a Roosting House
ADVENTURE SCALE: 2

The basics: Most people think of putting up birdhouses in spring, but you can put them out in winter too. Then birds will have a place to roost (sleep and rest) during cold days and nights. It's a great way to offer them protection.

Challenge: Offer a feeder near the roosting house. Then the birds won't have to travel far for food. Make sure you keep it filled throughout winter.

Did you know: Flying squirrels will also use boxes to roost in all winter long. So hang one up—you never know what you'll attract.

❏ 46: Make Something for the County Fair
ADVENTURE SCALE: 3

The basics: Almost every county in the country offers up the chance to enter exhibits into the county fair. However, fairs are in the summer, and this is a really busy time for most people. So take the chance to look at a fair book now (look online or check with your county extension) to see what you could be making for summer. Some of the common things you can enter in fairs include birdhouses, sketches, sewing projects, and mosaics. So start planning, and make it a fun family challenge and activity.

Challenge: Go outside of your comfort zone. Perhaps you like to draw but you don't take pictures. Use this opportunity to try a new hobby. Many community recreation departments have classes you can try. Find one that will help you make something for a county fair entry.

Did you know: Not only can you win ribbons for your entries into the fair, but many communities even pay you money as well!

47: Visit an Indoor Garden

ADVENTURE SCALE: 2

The basics: In some areas, people use a technique called aquaponics to grow crops. This involves fish and raised beds, and it's a very cool concept. There are more and more of these places every year, so see if you can find one in your area.

Challenge: Volunteer at an aquaponic location to see if you can help harvest the crops. Many are looking for volunteers, and it's a good learning experience. You could volunteer for a day or on a regular basis.

Did you know: Microgreens grow easily indoors and it only takes a couple of weeks. They are also good for you, and you can throw them on a salad. Pick up some seeds and try it yourself.

48: Learn to Use a Compass

ADVENTURE SCALE: 3

The basics: It seems like a compass should be easy to use, right? Well it is once you master it, but it takes a little bit of practice. The most important thing to remember is to hold it nice and steady.

Challenge: Take your compass out in the field on a hike and use it to find your way around. You'll soon see how it comes in handy.

Did you know: A compass works by aligning itself with the Earth's natural magnetic field. It always points in the direction of the field. Pretty cool, huh?

ZOOS AND AQUARIUMS

Zoos and aquariums are some of the most popular destinations for families. It's no wonder why—they showcase the world's amazing biodiversity, capture the imagination, and generate a lifelong interest in nature. The really good zoos and aquariums go beyond just highlighting animals. They also foster meaningful conservation work on a local and global scale. So check out and support those near you.

Who? These destinations are great for all ages. Often, the organizations even offer discount rates for youngsters, so even the smallest of naturalists will enjoy a visit to a zoo or an aquarium. Look for educational programs and day camps throughout the year. Some zoos and aquariums even offer internships for high school students.

What? Zoos and aquariums have educational exhibits, but they also provide critical conservation efforts, including captive breeding of numerous endangered species. Ask about what kind of efforts are involved in your area and how you might be able to help. Often zoos and aquariums will have special events where you get more of a behind-the-scenes look. If you get this opportunity, take it.

When? Winter can be a great time to visit zoos and aquariums. A few animals might be moved into indoor enclosures, but some other animals will become more active as the weather turns cooler. Indoor aquariums can keep you in touch with nature all winter long too. Plan ahead and you might be able to catch feeding time for some of the species.

Where? While many of the most famous zoos and aquariums are found in larger cities, smaller-scale operations can be equally as impressive. Look to your state or city visitor center to be your guide, and look for these types of places when you're traveling too.

Why? Zoos and aquariums offer close views of some of nature's most fascinating critters. Most of us don't live in areas that have a lot of these creatures naturally. Where else can you learn about so many different animals in such a short amount of time?

Tips and Tricks
Many zoos and aquariums offer seasonal discount rates. Visiting in the winter might just save you a buck or two. You can also gather up a bunch of friends and get a group rate in some instances.

49: Shop for Seeds

ADVENTURE SCALE: 1

The basics: Garden centers might not have plants available (except for house plants), but they will have seeds out. It's never too early to shop for seeds. Go on a particularly cold day when you need a pick-me-up. You can shop for seeds even if you won't be planting them for months.

Challenge: Create a map of your garden and put down where you want to plant certain varieties. Read the back of the seed packets and make notes as to how long they need to grow, what kind of light they require, and so on. Then come spring, you'll be ahead of the game.

Did you know: House plants really are a good way to scratch that gardening itch. Try an African violet or pick up a cactus. Explore your local garden center to see the different possibilities.

50: Dream about Spring

ADVENTURE SCALE: 1

The basics: Dreaming is fun. Even if it's in single digits outside, you can still think about what you'd like to be doing come spring. Make a "must-do" prioritized list for spring. Then on the first warm day you get, start crossing things off your list.

Challenge: Put together a "first day of spring" party. Yes, it's not spring yet, but you'll need to send out the invites and get everything planned in January and February. Chances are, you aren't the only one waiting for spring. You'll probably get a great turnout!

Did you know: Just getting a little sunshine (vitamin D) and dreaming of sunny days ahead can instantly perk you up. And if that doesn't work, make some lemonade or something else you normally do in warm weather.

Resources

When it comes to getting kids involved in nature, these nonprofit organizations are top-notch. Look online for how to get involved in some of their large campaigns or search for groups in your area that they work with.

Children & Nature Network
Author Richard Louv leads the Children & Nature Network and their Let's G.O.! campaign. This worthwhile group's goal is to get kids outside as much as possible. G.O. stands for "Get Outside," and this is exactly what they're hoping people will do during the month of April when this campaign is taking place. On their website, childrenandnature.ning.com, you can look up activities in your area. They don't just do things in April, though. Look up a family nature group to get involved in on their site or find other ways to help.

National Wildlife Federation
Go to nwf.org/Get-Outside to learn more about the National Wildlife Federation and their "Be Out There" campaign. The NWF has been dedicated to getting kids outside for decades. On their website they've compiled activities, ideas, and suggestions to keep you busy outside year-round. For more ideas, you can subscribe to their popular kids magazine, *Ranger Rick*. Take their advice. Be out there!

Nature Rocks
This group's goal is to inspire and empower families to play and explore in nature. Part of The Nature Conservancy, they have some great resources. Among them are seasonal activity guides you can download for free at naturerocks.org. On the site, you can also enter your zip code to find activities near you. This is a great organization with the motto "let's go explore." Get out there and follow their advice.

Roots and Shoots

Roots and Shoots is an organization that has been focusing on positive change for people, animals, and the environment for years. It focuses on youth and the powerful changes young-led campaigns can lead to. Go to rootsandshoots.org to look for a group to get involved with in your area. Or explore the "campaigns" area of the site to learn about worthwhile events to be part of.

Psst Kids!

Did you know Ken and Stacy are Nature Rocks Ambassadors? Yep, they sure are. They will help keep you informed of all the great ideas Nature Rocks comes out with. Keep an eye on destinationnature.net to learn about events, activity guides, and more.

Index

Spring

Summer

Fall

Winter

About the Authors

Photo by Jonathan Good/jgoodmedia.com

Stacy Tornio grew up in Oklahoma, though she's lived in Wisconsin for the last ten years. As editor of *Birds & Blooms* magazine, she is able to share her love of backyard nature with others. Stacy loves gardening (especially growing veggies) and is a master gardener in Milwaukee where she teaches youth gardening classes in the community. Along with her husband, Steve, Stacy enjoys watching her two children explore nature in their backyard and beyond. One of Stacy's favorite nature memories from childhood is having her own veggie stand at the local farmers' market with her brother.

Ken Keffer was born and raised in Wyoming. A vagabond naturalist, he's done a little bit of everything, from monitoring mice and vole populations and picking up carnivore scat in Grand Teton National Park to researching flying squirrels in the Tongass National Forest of southeast Alaska, and monitoring Bactrian camels in Mongolia's Great Gobi Strictly Protected Area. He's also worked as an environmental educator in Wyoming, northern New Mexico, coastal Maryland, and along the shores of Lake Erie in Ohio. Ken enjoys birding, floating on lazy rivers, and fly fishing in the mountains out west. One of Ken's favorite nature memories from childhood is building a fort at his grandparent's creek, which he lovingly referred to as Fort Fishy.

DestinationNature.net

ADVENTURES FROM BACKYARD TO MOUNTAINTOP